Taste *of* Home.

LAZY-DAY DINNERS, DESSERTS & MORE

TASTE OF HOME BOOKS • RDA ENTHUSIAST BRANDS, LLC • MILWAUKEE, WI

Visit us at **tasteofhome.com** for other
Taste of Home books and products.

International Standard Book Number:
979-8-88977-038-1

Chief Content Officer: Jason Burhmester
Content Director: Mark Hagen
Creative Director: Raeann Thompson
Senior Editor: Christine Rukavena
Editor: Hazel Wheaton
Senior Art Director: Courtney Lovetere
Assistant Art Directors: Carrie Peterson,
Jazmin Delgado
Manager, Production Design: Satyandra Raghav
Senior Print Publication Designer:
Jogesh Antony
Project Coordinator: Sierra Schuler
Production Artist: Nithya Venkatakrishnan
Deputy Editor, Copy Desk: Ann M. Walter
Copy Editors: Rayan Naqash, Suchismita Ukil

Cover Photography
Photographer: Dan Roberts
Set Stylist: Stacey Genaw
Food Stylist: Josh Rink

Pictured on front cover:
One-Pot Black Bean Enchilada Pasta, p. 130

Pictured on back cover:
Slow-Cooked Pork Stew, p. 147; Strawberry
Cheesecake Trifle, p. 235; Blackberry Sriracha
Chicken Sliders, p. 32;   Pressure-Cooker Green
Beans, p. 65; Beef Brisket Tacos, p. 148

Printed in China
1 3 5 7 9 10 8 6 4 2

PAGE
158

PAGE 246

PAGE 27

PAGE 181

PAGE 153

HANDY ICONS

Dozens of dishes inside are super short and freezer friendly.

5-INGREDIENT

Uses 5 or fewer ingredients (may call for water, salt, pepper, cooking oil or optional ingredients).

FREEZE

Includes freezing & reheating instructions.

LAZY-DAY...

APPLE-CRANBERRY
GRAINS, PAGE 12

LAZY-DAY
BREAKFASTS

FARMER'S CASSEROLE

Between family and friends, we average 375 visitors a year! This casserole is so handy—you can put it together the night before and let the flavors blend, then bake it in the morning.
—*Nancy Schmidt, Center, CO*

PREP: 10 MIN. + CHILLING • **BAKE:** 55 MIN. • **MAKES:** 6 SERVINGS

3 cups frozen shredded hash brown potatoes
¾ cup shredded Monterey Jack cheese
1 cup cubed fully cooked ham
¼ cup chopped green onions
4 large eggs
1 can (12 oz.) evaporated milk
¼ tsp. pepper
⅛ tsp. salt

1. Place potatoes in an 8-in. baking dish. Sprinkle with cheese, ham and onions. Whisk eggs, milk, pepper and salt; pour over top. Cover and refrigerate for several hours or overnight.
2. Remove from refrigerator 30 minutes before baking. Preheat oven to 350°. Bake, uncovered, until a knife inserted in the center comes out clean, 55-60 minutes.

1 SERVING 252 cal., 14g fat (7g sat. fat), 187mg chol., 531mg sod., 14g carb. (7g sugars, 1g fiber), 17g pro.

EASY DOES IT

Regular milk or half-and-half cream is a fine substitute for evaporated. This is a great casserole to make for guests on a gluten-free diet—no bread!

❄ BUTTERMILK PANCAKES

You just can't beat a basic buttermilk pancake for a down-home country breakfast. Paired with sausage and fresh fruit, these pancakes are just like the ones you get at Cracker Barrel.
—*Betty Abrey, Imperial, SK*

PREP: 10 MIN. • **COOK:** 5 MIN./BATCH • **MAKES:** 2½ DOZEN

4 cups all-purpose flour
¼ cup sugar
2 tsp. baking soda
2 tsp. salt
1½ tsp. baking powder
4 large eggs, room temperature
4 cups buttermilk

1. In a large bowl, combine the flour, sugar, baking soda, salt and baking powder. In another bowl, whisk the eggs and buttermilk until blended; stir into dry ingredients just until moistened.

2. Pour the batter by ¼ cupfuls onto a lightly greased hot griddle; turn when bubbles form on top. Cook until second side is golden brown.

FREEZE OPTION Freeze cooled pancakes between layers of waxed paper in a freezer container. To use, place pancakes on an ungreased baking sheet, cover with foil and reheat in a preheated 375° oven 6-10 minutes. Or place a stack of 3 pancakes on a microwave-safe plate and microwave on high until heated through, 45-90 seconds.

3 PANCAKES 270 cal., 3g fat (1g sat. fat), 89mg chol., 913mg sod., 48g carb. (11g sugars, 1g fiber), 11g pro.

PECAN APPLE PANCAKES To flour mixture, stir in 1¾ tsp. ground cinnamon, ¾ tsp. ground ginger, ¾ tsp. ground mace and ¾ tsp. ground cloves. To batter, fold in 2½ cups shredded peeled apples and ¾ cup chopped pecans.

BLUEBERRY PANCAKES Fold in 1 cup fresh or frozen blueberries.

BANANA WALNUT PANCAKES Fold in 2 finely chopped ripe bananas and ⅔ cup finely chopped walnuts.

❄ HONEY-OAT GRANOLA BARS

My husband and I enjoy these bars every day. It's a basic recipe to which you can add any of your favorite flavors. Try them with coconut or different kinds of chips, nuts and dried fruits.
—*Jean Boyce, New Ulm, MN*

PREP: 15 MIN. • **BAKE:** 15 MIN. + COOLING • **MAKES:** 3 DOZEN

- 4 cups quick-cooking oats
- 1 cup packed brown sugar
- 1 cup chopped salted peanuts
- 1 cup semisweet chocolate chips
- ½ cup sunflower kernels
- ¾ cup butter, melted
- ⅔ cup honey
- 1 tsp. vanilla extract

1. Preheat oven to 350°. In a large bowl, combine oats, brown sugar, peanuts, chocolate chips and sunflower kernels. Stir in melted butter, honey and vanilla until combined (mixture will be crumbly). Press into a greased parchment-lined 15x10x1-in. baking pan.
2. Bake until lightly browned, 15-20 minutes. Cool 15 minutes in pan on a wire rack; cut into bars. Cool completely before removing from pan.

FREEZE OPTION Transfer cooled bars to an airtight container. Cover and freeze for up to 2 months. To use, thaw bars at room temperature.

1 BAR 167 cal., 9g fat (4g sat. fat), 10mg chol., 54mg sod., 21g carb. (14g sugars, 2g fiber), 3g pro. **DIABETIC EXCHANGES** 1½ starch, 1½ fat.

NO-TURN OMELET

It's a snap to put together this colorful casserole. I like to make it a day ahead, then refrigerate and bake the next morning. With ingredients such as sausage, eggs, cheese and peppers, it tastes like a strata—except it uses crackers rather than the traditional bread cubes.

—Helen Clem, Creston, IA

PREP: 10 MIN. • **BAKE:** 45 MIN. • **MAKES:** 10 SERVINGS

8   large eggs, lightly beaten
2   cups cooked crumbled
    sausage or cubed fully
    cooked ham
2   cups cubed Velveeta
2   cups 2% milk
1   cup crushed saltines
    (about 24 crackers)
¼   cup chopped onion
¼   cup chopped green pepper
¼   cup chopped sweet
    red pepper
½   to 1 tsp. salt

1. In a large bowl, combine all ingredients. Pour into a greased shallow 3-qt. or 13x9-in. baking dish.

2. Bake, uncovered, at 350° until a knife inserted in the center comes out clean, for 45 minutes. Let stand for 5 minutes before serving.

NOTE This dish may be prepared in advance, covered and refrigerated overnight. Remove from the refrigerator 30 minutes before baking.

1 CUP 272 cal., 18g fat (8g sat. fat), 213mg chol., 767mg sod., 10g carb. (5g sugars, 0 fiber), 18g pro.

READER REVIEW
"We love this recipe. It is so easy and quick. I bake seasoned potato wedges at the same time. Just add a fruit salad or some sliced fruit, and dinner is ready! I find this to be a very flexible recipe. If I don't have, or prefer not to use, sausage, I can add extra veggies for a meatless version. It also works well with chopped ham or crumbled cooked bacon instead of sausage. It's great with the Velveeta as specified, but I also make it with shredded cheddar. Highly recommended!"
—MRS_T, TASTEOFHOME.COM

APPLE-CRANBERRY GRAINS

I made some changes to my diet in order to lose weight. My kids are skeptical when it comes to healthy food, but they adore these wholesome grains.
—*Sherisse Dawe, Black Diamond, AB*

PREP: 10 MIN. • **COOK:** 4 HOURS • **MAKES:** 16 SERVINGS

- 2 **medium apples, peeled and chopped**
- 1 **cup sugar**
- 1 **cup fresh cranberries**
- ½ **cup wheat berries**
- ½ **cup quinoa, rinsed**
- ½ **cup oat bran**
- ½ **cup medium pearl barley**
- ½ **cup chopped walnuts**
- ½ **cup packed brown sugar**
- 1½ **to 2 tsp. ground cinnamon**
- 6 **cups water**
   Optional toppings: Milk, sliced apples, dried cranberries and chopped walnuts

In a 4- or 5-qt. slow cooker, combine the first 11 ingredients. Cook, covered, on low until grains are tender, 4-5 hours. Serve with toppings as desired.

¾ CUP 180 cal., 3g fat (0 sat. fat), 0 chol., 3mg sod., 37g carb. (22g sugars, 4g fiber), 3g pro.

READER REVIEW
"Even my kids love this! The amount of sugar (or substitute whatever sweetener you'd like) is fine for a batch this large. Or don't use any and sweeten after cooking to your taste."
—SHERISSEY, TASTEOFHOME.COM

**STRAWBERRY
BANANA SMOOTHIES**

⑤ⱼ STRAWBERRY BANANA SMOOTHIES

Sometimes a simple, healthy smoothie is all you need to start your day out right. It also makes a fantastic afternoon pick-me-up when kids get home from school. Experiment with different types of milk and yogurt or add ice for a frosty texture.
—Taste of Home *Test Kitchen*

TAKES: 5 MIN. • **MAKES:** 2 SERVINGS

1½ cups fresh strawberries
1   medium banana, peeled, quartered and frozen
½   cup plain Greek yogurt
½   cup 2% milk
    Honey, optional

Place the first 4 ingredients in a blender; cover and process until blended. If desired, add honey to taste and garnish with additional strawberry and banana.
1½ CUPS 183 cal., 7g fat (4g sat. fat), 20mg chol., 65mg sod., 27g carb. (18g sugars, 4g fiber), 5g pro. **DIABETIC EXCHANGES** 1½ fruit, ½ reduced-fat milk.

PUMPKIN SPICE OATMEAL

There's nothing like a warm cup of oatmeal in the morning, and my spiced version works in a slow cooker. Store leftovers in the fridge.
—*Jordan Mason, Brookville, PA*

PREP: 10 MIN. • **COOK:** 5 HOURS • **MAKES:** 6 SERVINGS

1   can (15 oz.) pumpkin
1   cup steel-cut oats
3   Tbsp. brown sugar
1½ tsp. pumpkin pie spice
1   tsp. ground cinnamon
¾   tsp. salt
3   cups water
1½ cups 2% milk
    Optional toppings: Toasted chopped pecans, ground cinnamon, and additional brown sugar and milk

In a large bowl, combine the first 6 ingredients; stir in water and milk. Transfer to a greased 3-qt. slow cooker. Cook, covered, on low 5-6 hours or until oats are tender, stirring once. Serve with toppings as desired.
1 CUP 183 cal., 3g fat (1g sat. fat), 5mg chol., 329mg sod., 34g carb. (13g sugars, 5g fiber), 6g pro. **DIABETIC EXCHANGES** 2 starch, ½ fat.

FRENCH TOAST CASSEROLE

I sprinkle a cinnamon-sugar topping on my easy oven version of French toast. I love the fact that I can assemble it the night before and save time in the morning.

—*Sharyn Adams, Crawfordsville, IN*

PREP: 15 MIN. + CHILLING • **BAKE:** 45 MIN. • **MAKES:** 12 SERVINGS

1 **loaf (1 lb.) French bread, cut into 1-in. cubes**
8 **large eggs, lightly beaten**
3 **cups 2% milk**
4 **tsp. sugar**
1 **tsp. vanilla extract**
¾ **tsp. salt**

TOPPING
2 **Tbsp. butter**
3 **Tbsp. sugar**
2 **tsp. ground cinnamon**
   Maple syrup, optional

1. Place bread cubes in a greased 13x9-in. baking dish. In a large bowl, whisk the eggs, milk, sugar, vanilla and salt. Pour over bread. Cover and refrigerate for 8 hours or overnight.
2. Remove from refrigerator 30 minutes before baking. Preheat oven to 350°. Dot with butter. Combine sugar and cinnamon; sprinkle over the top.
3. Cover and bake until a knife inserted in the center comes out clean, 45-50 minutes. Let stand for 5 minutes. Serve with maple syrup if desired.

1 SERVING 223 cal., 7g fat (3g sat. fat), 151mg chol., 484mg sod., 29g carb. (9g sugars, 1g fiber), 11g pro

TEST KITCHEN TIP

You can use flavored loaves in this dish, such as cinnamon-raisin bread or cranberry-walnut bread. Make sure the bread is dense instead of fluffy, and that it is slightly stale. If you need to dry it out quickly, cube your bread and bake in a 200° oven for 10-15 minutes.

⑤ ❄ EGG BURRITOS

Zap one of these frozen burritos in the microwave and you'll stave off hunger all morning. This recipe is my family's favorite combo, but I sometimes use breakfast sausage instead of bacon.
—*Audra Niederman, Aberdeen, SD*

TAKES: 25 MIN. • **MAKES:** 10 BURRITOS

12 **bacon strips, chopped**
12 **large eggs**
½ **tsp. salt**
¼ **tsp. pepper**
10 **flour tortillas (8 in.), warmed**
1½ **cups shredded cheddar cheese**
4 **green onions, thinly sliced**

1. In a large cast-iron or other heavy skillet, cook bacon until crisp; drain on paper towels. Remove all but 1-2 Tbsp. drippings from pan.
2. Whisk together the eggs, salt and pepper. Heat skillet over medium heat; pour in egg mixture. Cook and stir until eggs are thickened and no liquid egg remains; remove from heat.
3. Spoon about ¼ cup egg mixture onto center of each tortilla; sprinkle with cheese, bacon and green onions. Roll into burritos.

FREEZE OPTION Cool eggs before making burritos. Individually wrap burritos in paper towels and foil; freeze in an airtight container. To use, remove foil; place paper towel-wrapped burrito on a microwave-safe plate. Microwave on high until heated through, turning once. Let stand 15 seconds.

1 BURRITO 376 cal., 20g fat (8g sat. fat), 251mg chol., 726mg sod., 29g carb. (0 sugars, 2g fiber), 19g pro.

EASY DOES IT

Breakfast burritos can be a smart choice to start the day because they include a good amount of protein. To make these healthier, use whole wheat tortillas, skip the bacon, reduce the cheese and add your favorite sauteed veggies.

🔟 APPLE YOGURT PARFAITS

Get the morning started right with this super simple four-ingredient parfait. Try chunky or flavored applesauce for easy variations.
—*Rebekah Radewahn, Wauwatosa, WI*

TAKES: 10 MIN. • **MAKES:** 4 SERVINGS

1   cup sweetened applesauce
     Dash ground nutmeg
½   cup granola with raisins
1⅓ cups vanilla yogurt

In a small bowl, combine the applesauce and nutmeg. Spoon 1 Tbsp. granola into each of 4 parfait glasses. Layer each with ⅓ cup yogurt and ¼ cup applesauce; sprinkle with remaining granola. Serve immediately.

1 PARFAIT 158 cal., 2g fat (1g sat. fat), 4mg chol., 70mg sod., 30g carb. (24g sugars, 1g fiber), 5g pro. **DIABETIC EXCHANGES** 2 starch.

🔟 SPINACH SMOOTHIES

Get a jump-start on all the nutrients you need by starting your day with this smoothie. Use nondairy milk and yogurt if you prefer.
—Taste of Home *Test Kitchen*

TAKES: 10 MIN. • **MAKES:** 4 SERVINGS

¾   cup 2% milk
½   cup plain Greek yogurt
1   cup ice cubes
1   cup fresh spinach
1   ripe medium banana
1   cup cubed fresh pineapple,
     frozen

In a blender, combine all ingredients; cover and process for 30 seconds or until smooth.

1 CUP 104 cal., 4g fat (2g sat. fat), 11mg chol., 58mg sod., 16g carb. (11g sugars, 2g fiber), 3g pro. **DIABETIC EXCHANGES** 1 starch, ½ fat.

READER REVIEW
"Very good—not too sweet, and not too strong of a spinach taste. Will make again."
—CHRISTINE0964, TASTEOFHOME.COM

APPLE YOGURT
PARFAITS

SLOW-COOKER CRAB
& GREEN ONION DIP,
PAGE 31

LAZY-DAY
PARTY FARE

🄯 PIZZA PINWHEELS

These little treats taste a lot like a rolled-up pizza. With crispy pepperoni and lots of mozzarella and Parmesan, what's not to love?

—*Dorothy Smith, El Dorado, AR*

TAKES: 25 MIN. • **MAKES:** 8 APPETIZERS

1 tube (13.8 oz.) refrigerated pizza crust
1 cup shredded part-skim mozzarella cheese
¼ cup grated Parmesan cheese
1 cup chopped pepperoni (about 64 slices)
½ cup spaghetti sauce, warmed, optional

1. Preheat oven to 400°. On a lightly floured surface, roll dough into a 16x10-in. rectangle. Sprinkle with cheeses and pepperoni.

2. Roll up jelly-roll style, starting with a long side. Cut into 2-in. slices. Place cut side down in a greased 15x10x1-in. baking pan; lightly press down to flatten.

3. Bake for 8-10 minutes or until golden brown. Serve with spaghetti sauce if desired.

1 PINWHEEL 265 cal., 13g fat (5g sat. fat), 26mg chol., 776mg sod., 24g carb. (3g sugars, 1g fiber), 12g pro.

EASY DOES IT

Like most other pizza-inspired recipes, these pinwheels can be customized to match your family's favorite pizza toppings. Try different meats like cooked sausage or Canadian bacon, plus veggies like chopped green pepper, red onion, mushrooms or olives.

**MOCK CHAMPAGNE
PUNCH**

⑤ MOCK CHAMPAGNE PUNCH

I have tried many punch recipes, but I keep coming back to this pretty one that's nonalcoholic.
—*Betty Claycomb, Alverton, PA*

TAKES: 10 MIN. • **MAKES:** 16 SERVINGS

1 qt. white grape juice, chilled
1 qt. ginger ale, chilled
   Strawberries or raspberries

Combine grape juice and ginger ale; pour into a punch bowl or glasses. Garnish with berries.

½ CUP 58 cal., 0 fat (0 sat. fat), 0 chol., 8mg sod., 14g carb. (14g sugars, 0 fiber), 0 pro.

HOT WING DIP

Since I usually have all the ingredients on hand for this recipe, this is a terrific go-to snack when entertaining friends and family.
—*Coleen Corner, Grove City, PA*

PREP: 10 MIN. • **COOK:** 1 HOUR • **MAKES:** 4½ CUPS

2 cups shredded cooked chicken
1 pkg. (8 oz.) cream cheese, cubed
2 cups shredded cheddar cheese
1 cup ranch salad dressing
½ cup Louisiana-style hot sauce
   Minced fresh parsley, optional
   Tortilla chips and celery sticks

In a 3- or 4-qt. slow cooker, mix the first 5 ingredients.
Cook, covered, on low for 1-2 hours or until cheese is melted. If desired, sprinkle with parsley. Serve with the tortilla chips and celery.

¼ CUP 186 cal., 16g fat (7g sat. fat), 43mg chol., 235mg sod., 2g carb. (1g sugars, 0 fiber), 8g pro.

SLOW-COOKER CAPONATA

This Italian eggplant dip preps quickly and actually gets better as it stands. Serve it warm or at room temperature. Try adding a little leftover caponata to scrambled eggs for a savory breakfast.

—*Nancy Beckman, Helena, MT*

PREP: 20 MIN. • **COOK:** 5 HOURS • **MAKES:** 6 CUPS

2 medium eggplants, cut into ½-in. pieces
1 medium onion, chopped
1 can (14½ oz.) diced tomatoes, undrained
12 garlic cloves, sliced
½ cup dry red wine
3 Tbsp. olive oil
2 Tbsp. red wine vinegar
4 tsp. capers, undrained
5 bay leaves
1½ tsp. salt
¼ tsp. coarsely ground pepper
French bread baguette slices, toasted
Optional: Sliced fresh basil leaves, toasted pine nuts and additional olive oil

Place first 11 ingredients in a 6-qt. slow cooker (do not stir). Cook, covered, on high for 3 hours. Stir gently; replace cover. Cook on high 2 hours longer or until the vegetables are tender. Cool slightly; discard bay leaves. Serve with toasted baguette slices, adding toppings as desired.

¼ CUP 34 cal., 2g fat (0 sat. fat), 0 chol., 189mg sod., 4g carb. (2g sugars, 2g fiber), 1g pro.

EASY DOES IT

For easy entertaining, serve warm directly from the slow cooker or at room temperature.

SLOW-COOKER CRAB & GREEN ONION DIP

This creamy dip reminds me of my dad, who took us crabbing as kids. Our fingers were always tired after those excursions, but eating the fresh crab was worth it.
—*Nancy Zimmerman, Cape May Court House, NJ*

PREP: 10 MIN. • **COOK:** 3 HOURS • **MAKES:** 4 CUPS

3 pkg. (8 oz. each) cream cheese, cubed
2 cans (6 oz. each) lump crabmeat, drained
4 green onions, chopped
¼ cup 2% milk
2 tsp. prepared horseradish
2 tsp. Worcestershire sauce
¼ tsp. salt
   Baked pita chips or assorted fresh vegetables

In a greased 3-qt. slow cooker, combine first 7 ingredients. Cook, covered, on low for 3-4 hours or until heated through, stirring occasionally. Serve with chips or fresh vegetables.
¼ CUP 167 cal., 15g fat (8g sat. fat), 68mg chol., 324mg sod., 2g carb. (2g sugars, 0 fiber), 7g pro.

READER REVIEW
"This recipe was fantastic! I prepped the night before and stuck it in the crock the next day. It was a huge hit. Next time, I'm going to have to triple the recipe. This is a keeper."
—SPOILEDBASHER, TASTEOFHOME.COM

❄ BLACKBERRY SRIRACHA CHICKEN SLIDERS

Dump everything in a slow cooker and then watch these spicy-sweet sliders become an instant party-time classic.

—Julie Peterson, Crofton, MD

PREP: 20 MIN. • **COOK:** 5 HOURS • **MAKES:** 1 DOZEN

1 jar (10 oz.) seedless blackberry spreadable fruit
¼ cup ketchup
¼ cup balsamic vinegar
¼ cup Sriracha chili sauce
2 Tbsp. molasses
1 Tbsp. Dijon mustard
¼ tsp. salt
3½ lbs. bone-in chicken thighs
1 large onion, thinly sliced
4 garlic cloves, minced
12 pretzel mini buns, split
  Additional Sriracha chili sauce
  Leaf lettuce and tomato slices

1. In a 4- or 5-qt. slow cooker, stir together first 7 ingredients. Add the chicken, onion and garlic. Toss to combine.

2. Cook, covered, on low until chicken is tender, 5-6 hours.

3. Remove chicken. When cool enough to handle, remove bones and skin; discard. Shred meat with 2 forks. Reserve 3 cups cooking juices; discard remaining juices. Skim fat from reserved juices. Return chicken and reserved juices to slow cooker; heat through. Using a slotted spoon, serve on pretzel buns. Drizzle with additional chili sauce; top with lettuce and tomato.

FREEZE OPTION Freeze cooled chicken mixture in freezer containers. To use, partially thaw in refrigerator overnight. Heat through in a covered saucepan, stirring occasionally; add a little broth if necessary.

1 SLIDER 352 cal., 14g fat (3g sat. fat), 63mg chol., 413mg sod., 35g carb. (12g sugars, 1g fiber), 21g pro.

WARM BROCCOLI CHEESE DIP

When my family gathers for a party, this flavorful, creamy dip is served. Everyone loves its zip from the jalapeno pepper and the crunch of the broccoli.

—Barbara Maiol, Conyers, GA

PREP: 15 MIN. • **COOK:** 2½ HOURS • **MAKES:** 5½ CUPS

2   jars (8 oz. each) process cheese sauce
1   can (10¾ oz.) condensed cream of chicken soup, undiluted
3   cups frozen chopped broccoli, thawed and drained
½   lb. fresh mushrooms, chopped
2   Tbsp. chopped seeded jalapeno pepper
    Assorted fresh vegetables

In a 1½-qt. slow cooker, combine cheese sauce and soup. Cover and cook on low for 30 minutes or until the cheese is melted, stirring occasionally. Stir in broccoli, mushrooms and jalapeno. Cover and cook on low until the vegetables are tender, 2-3 hours. Serve with assorted fresh vegetables.

NOTE Wear disposable gloves when cutting hot peppers; the oils can burn skin. Avoid touching your face.

¼ CUP 47 cal., 3g fat (2g sat. fat), 7mg chol., 277mg sod., 3g carb. (1g sugars, 1g fiber), 2g pro.

READER REVIEW

"Broccoli dips are a favorite in our home, as are many broccoli dishes. I loved the zip and zing from the hot peppers. I served it with crudites and cubed hearty bread (pumpernickel, Jewish rye and a good crusty sourdough). I recommend the recipe for family events or gatherings, tailgating, church events, as a food gift when invited out, or as a gift on a holiday with the recipe and ingredients tucked into a basket."

LILLIANLBRK, TASTEOFHOME.COM

🔵 ❄ MARMALADE MEATBALLS

We had a potluck at work, so I started cooking these meatballs in the morning. By lunchtime they were ready. They were a big hit!
—*Jeanne Kiss, Greensburg, PA*

PREP: 10 MIN. • **COOK:** 4 HOURS • **MAKES:** ABOUT 5 DOZEN

1 **bottle (16 oz.) Catalina salad dressing**
1 **cup orange marmalade**
3 **Tbsp. Worcestershire sauce**
½ **tsp. crushed red pepper flakes**
1 **pkg. (32 oz.) frozen fully cooked home-style meatballs, thawed**

In a 3-qt. slow cooker, combine the salad dressing, marmalade, Worcestershire sauce and pepper flakes. Stir in meatballs. Cover and cook on low for 4-5 hours or until heated through.

FREEZE OPTION Freeze cooled meatball mixture in freezer containers. To use, partially thaw in refrigerator overnight. Microwave, covered, on high in a microwave-safe dish until heated through, gently stirring; add water if necessary.

1 MEATBALL 73 cal., 4g fat (1g sat. fat), 12mg chol., 126mg sod., 6g carb. (5g sugars, 0 fiber), 2g pro.

EASY PARTY MEATBALLS Omit first 4 ingredients. Combine 1 bottle (14 oz.) ketchup, ¼ cup A.1. steak sauce, 1 Tbsp. minced garlic and 1 tsp. Dijon mustard in slow cooker; stir in meatballs. Cook as directed.

51 ❄ HAM & BRIE PASTRIES

Growing up, I loved pocket pastries. Now with a busy family, I need quick bites, and my spin on the classic ham and cheese delivers at snack or supper time.
—*Jenn Tidwell, Fair Oaks, CA*

TAKES: 30 MIN. • **MAKES:** 16 PASTRIES

1 sheet frozen puff pastry, thawed
⅓ cup apricot preserves
4 slices deli ham, quartered
8 oz. Brie cheese, cut into 16 pieces

1. Preheat oven to 400°. On a lightly floured surface, unfold the puff pastry. Roll pastry to a 12-in. square; cut into sixteen 3-in. squares. Place 1 tsp. preserves in center of each square; top with the ham, folding as necessary, and cheese. Overlap 2 opposite corners of pastry over filling; pinch tightly to seal.

2. Place pastries on a parchment-lined baking sheet. Bake 15-20 minutes or until golden brown. Cool on pan 5 minutes before serving. If desired, serve with additional apricot preserves.

FREEZE OPTION Freeze cooled pastries in a freezer container, separating layers with waxed paper. To use, reheat pastries on a baking sheet in a preheated 400° oven until heated through.

1 APPETIZER 144 cal., 8g fat (3g sat. fat), 17mg chol., 192mg sod., 13g carb. (3g sugars, 1g fiber), 5g pro.

COQUITO

COQUITO

An all-time family favorite, this creamy adult beverage features cream of coconut blended with cloves, cinnamon, vanilla and rum.
—*Evelyn Robles, Oak Creek, WI*

PREP: 15 MIN. + CHILLING • **MAKES:** 8 SERVINGS

1 can (15 oz.) cream of coconut
1 can (14 oz.) sweetened condensed milk
1 can (12 oz.) evaporated milk
½ cup water
1 tsp. vanilla extract
½ tsp. ground cinnamon
¼ tsp. ground cloves
1 cup rum

Place the first 7 ingredients in a blender; cover and process until blended. Refrigerate until chilled. Stir in rum before serving.

¾ CUP 488 cal., 17g fat (12g sat. fat), 30mg chol., 132mg sod., 63g carb. (63g sugars, 0 fiber), 7g pro.

5i SLOW-COOKED SMOKIES

I like to include these little smokies smothered in barbecue sauce on all my appetizer buffets since they're popular with both children and adults.
—*Sundra Hauck, Bogalusa, LA*

PREP: 5 MIN. • **COOK:** 5 HOURS • **MAKES:** 8 SERVINGS

1 pkg. (14 oz.) miniature smoked sausages
1 bottle (28 oz.) barbecue sauce
1¼ cups water
3 Tbsp. Worcestershire sauce
3 Tbsp. steak sauce
½ tsp. pepper

In a 3-qt. slow cooker, combine all ingredients. Cover and cook on low for 5-6 hours or until heated through. Serve with a slotted spoon.

1 SERVING 331 cal., 14g fat (5g sat. fat), 32mg chol., 1694mg sod., 44g carb. (35g sugars, 1g fiber), 7g pro.

FRUITY HORSERADISH CREAM CHEESE

Typically called a Jezebel sauce, this sweet, fruity topping has an underlying bite from horseradish. It pairs well with cream cheese, but you could also try it over grilled pork and chicken.

—*Rita Reifenstein, Evans City, PA*

TAKES: 10 MIN. • **MAKES:** 1⅓ CUPS

1 pkg. (8 oz.) fat-free cream cheese
⅓ cup apple jelly, warmed
1 Tbsp. prepared horseradish
1½ tsp. ground mustard
⅓ cup apricot spreadable fruit
Assorted crackers

Place cream cheese on a serving plate. In a small microwave-safe bowl, heat jelly until warmed. Stir in horseradish and mustard until blended. Stir in spreadable fruit; spoon over cream cheese. Serve with crackers. Refrigerate leftovers.

2 TBSP. 73 cal., 0 fat (0 sat. fat), 2mg chol., 128mg sod., 14g carb. (11g sugars, 0 fiber), 3g pro. **DIABETIC EXCHANGES** 1 starch.

DID YOU KNOW?

Jezebel sauce is named after the biblical figure Queen Jezebel because of its signature sweet and spicy flavor. It usually gets sweetness from apple or pineapple preserves, and is balanced by heat from horseradish or mustard.

❄ SLOW-COOKER MARINATED MUSHROOMS

Here's a terrific healthy addition to any buffet spread. Mushrooms and pearl onions seasoned with herbs, balsamic and red wine are terrific on their own or alongside a tenderloin roast.
—*Courtney Wilson, Fresno, CA*

PREP: 15 MIN. • **COOK:** 6 HOURS • **MAKES:** 5 CUPS

2 lbs. medium fresh mushrooms
1 pkg. (14.4 oz.) frozen pearl onions, thawed
4 garlic cloves, minced
2 cups reduced-sodium beef broth
½ cup dry red wine
3 Tbsp. balsamic vinegar
3 Tbsp. olive oil
1 tsp. salt
1 tsp. dried basil
½ tsp. dried thyme
½ tsp. pepper
¼ tsp. crushed red pepper flakes

Place mushrooms, onions and garlic in a 5- or 6-qt. slow cooker. In a small bowl, whisk remaining ingredients; pour over mushrooms. Cook, covered, on low 6-8 hours or until mushrooms are tender.

FREEZE OPTION Freeze the cooled mushrooms and juices in freezer containers. To use, partially thaw in refrigerator overnight. Microwave, covered, on high in a microwave-safe dish until heated through, stirring gently and adding broth or water if necessary.

¼ CUP 42 cal., 2g fat (0 sat. fat), 1mg chol., 165mg sod., 4g carb. (2g sugars, 0 fiber), 1g pro.

READER REVIEW
"Great flavors. Perfect with steak."
—STEVE, TASTEOFHOME.COM

SALMON SALAD-STUFFED ENDIVE LEAVES

Salmon creates an elegant appetizer in this vibrant recipe. It's simple to prepare and can even be made ahead of time.
—Melissa Carafa, Broomall, PA

TAKES: 15 MIN. • **MAKES:** 14 PIECES

1 **salmon fillet (6 oz.), cooked and flaked**
¼ **cup tartar sauce**
2 **tsp. capers**
1 **tsp. snipped fresh dill**
¼ **tsp. lemon-pepper seasoning**
1 **head Belgian endive (about 5 oz.), separated into leaves**

In a small bowl, combine salmon, tartar sauce, capers, dill and lemon pepper. Spoon about 2 tsp. salmon salad onto each endive leaf. If desired, garnish with additional dill. Refrigerate until serving.
1 PIECE 42 cal., 3g fat (1g sat. fat), 9mg chol., 60mg sod., 2g carb. (0 sugars, 1g fiber), 3g pro.

---

⑤① ORANGE PARTY PUNCH

This citrus punch was served at every birthday party I had when I was growing up. Now I prepare it for my kids. You can float orange slices between the scoops of sherbet for extra flair.
—Brenda Rupert, Clyde, OH

TAKES: 10 MIN. • **MAKES:** 5½ QT.

1 **can (12 oz.) frozen orange juice concentrate, thawed**
2 **liters lemon-lime soda, chilled**
1 **can (46 oz.) pineapple juice, chilled**
1 **qt. orange or pineapple sherbet**

Prepare orange juice according to package directions; pour into a punch bowl. Stir in soda and pineapple juice. Top with scoops of sherbet. Serve immediately.
1 CUP 142 cal., 1g fat (0 sat. fat), 2mg chol., 24mg sod., 34g carb. (32g sugars, 0 fiber), 1g pro.

**SALMON SALAD-STUFFED
ENDIVE LEAVES**

PRESSURE-COOKER
GREEN BEANS, PAGE 65

LAZY-DAY SIDES

TUNA MACARONI SALAD

Pack this classic salad for a picnic or workplace lunch. For best results, keep the salad in the fridge overnight to allow flavors to blend.
—Taste of Home *Test Kitchen*

PREP: 20 MIN. + CHILLING • **MAKES:** 10 SERVINGS

2 cups uncooked elbow macaroni
1 cup mayonnaise
¼ cup sweet pickle relish
½ tsp. salt
¼ tsp. pepper
1 cup frozen peas, thawed
½ cup chopped sweet onion
½ cup chopped celery
1 can (5 oz.) light tuna in water, drained and flaked
3 hard-boiled large eggs, chopped

1. Cook macaroni according to package directions; drain and rinse with cold water. Cool completely.
2. For dressing, combine mayonnaise, relish, salt and pepper. In a large bowl, combine peas, onion, celery, tuna, eggs and macaroni. Add dressing; gently toss to coat. Refrigerate until serving.

¾ CUP 255 cal., 18g fat (3g sat. fat), 69mg chol., 352mg sod., 16g carb. (3g sugars, 1g fiber), 7g pro.

READER REVIEW
"This a great summer salad that you can serve as a meal. It makes a smaller amount than most pasta salads, so it is nice for small households."
—PAGE RD, TASTEOFHOME.COM

MUSHROOM
WILD RICE

MUSHROOM WILD RICE

This is one of my favorite recipes from my mother. With only seven ingredients, it's quick to assemble in the morning before I leave for work. By the time I get home, mouthwatering aromas have filled the house.
—*Bob Malchow, Monon, IN*

PREP: 5 MIN. • **COOK:** 3 HOURS • **MAKES:** 12 SERVINGS

2¼ cups water
1 can (10½ oz.) condensed beef consomme, undiluted
1 can (10½ oz.) condensed French onion soup, undiluted
3 cans (4 oz. each) mushroom stems and pieces, drained
½ cup butter, melted
1 cup uncooked brown rice
1 cup uncooked wild rice

In a 3-qt. slow cooker, combine all ingredients. Cover and cook on low until rice is tender, 3-4 hours.
¾ CUP 192 cal., 9g fat (5g sat. fat), 21mg chol., 437mg sod., 24g carb. (2g sugars, 2g fiber), 5g pro.

READER REVIEW
"Excellent dish. I used a 6-qt. slow cooker, so I doubled the recipe, and it was great! I will definitely make this again. I might try adding some precooked sausage to it the next time. Don't be afraid to make this one!"
—BAHSTONFRN_IA, TASTEOFHOME.COM

CHEESY SPINACH

My daughter often serves this cheese and spinach blend at church suppers. Even people who don't usually eat spinach like this flavorful dish once they try it. There are never any leftovers.
—*Frances Moore, Decatur, IL*

PREP: 10 MIN. • **COOK:** 5 HOURS • **MAKES:** 8 SERVINGS

2 pkg. (10 oz. each) frozen chopped spinach, thawed and squeezed dry
2 cups 4% cottage cheese
1½ cups cubed Velveeta
3 large eggs, lightly beaten
¼ cup butter, cubed
¼ cup all-purpose flour
1 tsp. salt

In a large bowl, combine all ingredients. Pour into a greased 3-qt. slow cooker. Cover and cook on high for 1 hour. Reduce heat to low; cook 4-5 hours longer or until a knife inserted in center comes out clean.
¾ CUP 230 cal., 15g fat (9g sat. fat), 121mg chol., 855mg sod., 9g carb. (4g sugars, 1g fiber), 14g pro.

🅢 BACON PEA SALAD

My husband absolutely loves peas. My middle son isn't the biggest fan, but he loves bacon. So I decided to combine the two, and it was perfect! This salad is an awesome side dish, especially for barbecues.
—*Angela Lively, Conroe, TX*

PREP: 10 MIN. + CHILLING • **MAKES:** 6 SERVINGS

4   cups frozen peas
    (about 16 oz.), thawed
½   cup shredded sharp
    cheddar cheese
½   cup ranch salad dressing
⅓   cup chopped red onion
¼   tsp. salt
¼   tsp. pepper
4   bacon strips, cooked
    and crumbled

Combine the first 6 ingredients; toss to coat. Refrigerate, covered, at least 30 minutes. Stir in bacon before serving.

¾ CUP 218 cal., 14g fat (4g sat. fat), 17mg chol., 547mg sod., 14g carb. (6g sugars, 4g fiber), 9g pro.

CREAMY COLESLAW

For me, this is the best coleslaw recipe because a package of shredded cabbage and carrots really cuts down on prep time. This coleslaw recipe is great for potlucks or to serve to your family on a busy weeknight.
—*Renee Endress, Galva, IL*

TAKES: 10 MIN. • **MAKES:** 6 SERVINGS

1   pkg. (14 oz.) coleslaw mix
¾   cup mayonnaise
⅓   cup sour cream
¼   cup sugar
¾   tsp. seasoned salt
½   tsp. ground mustard
¼   tsp. celery salt

Place coleslaw mix in a large bowl. In a small bowl, combine remaining ingredients; stir until blended. Pour over coleslaw mix and toss to coat. Refrigerate until serving.

¾ CUP 256 cal., 23g fat (5g sat. fat), 19mg chol., 398mg sod., 13g carb. (11g sugars, 2g fiber), 1g pro.

BACON PEA
SALAD

SOUTHERN POTATO SALAD

This potato salad with a southern twist is perfect for a church supper or potluck. The pickles add an extra sweetness.
—*Gene Pitts, Wilsonville, AL*

PREP: 30 MIN. + CHILLING • **MAKES:** 8 SERVINGS

5 **medium potatoes, peeled and cubed**
6 **hard-boiled large eggs, chopped**
½ **cup thinly sliced green onions**
¼ **cup chopped sweet pickles**
1 **tsp. prepared mustard**
1 **tsp. celery seed**
1 **cup mayonnaise**
 Salt and pepper to taste

Place potatoes in a large saucepan; add water to cover. Bring to a boil. Reduce heat; cook, uncovered, for 10-15 minutes or until tender. Drain; refrigerate until cold. Add eggs, onions and pickles; toss well. Stir in mustard, celery seed and mayonnaise. Season with salt and pepper; mix well. Refrigerate until cold.

¾ CUP 377 cal., 26g fat (4g sat. fat), 169mg chol., 275mg sod., 28g carb. (5g sugars, 2g fiber), 8g pro.

DID YOU KNOW?

Celery seed is a classic addition to seafood dishes, salads and pickles. The seeds are herbaceous, crunchy and slightly bitter. They come from a type of flavorful Asian celery.

❄ SLOW-COOKER POTLUCK BEANS

It was the morning of our family potluck and I still needed something to bring. I threw together this recipe while drinking my morning coffee. By the end of the gathering, the beans were all gone and someone had even washed the slow cooker for me!
—*Mary Anne Thygesen, Portland, OR*

PREP: 10 MIN. • **COOK:** 4 HOURS • **MAKES:** 18 SERVINGS

1 **cup brewed coffee**
½ **cup packed brown sugar**
¼ **cup spicy brown mustard**
2 **Tbsp. molasses**
2 **cans (16 oz. each) butter beans**
2 **cans (16 oz. each) kidney beans**
2 **cans (16 oz. each) navy beans**

In a greased 3- or 4-qt. slow cooker, mix first 4 ingredients. Rinse and drain beans; stir into coffee mixture. Cook, covered, on low until flavors are blended, 4-5 hours.

FREEZE OPTION Freeze cooled beans in freezer containers. To use, partially thaw in refrigerator overnight. Heat through in a covered saucepan, stirring occasionally; add water if necessary.
½ CUP 183 cal., 0 fat (0 sat. fat), 0 chol., 403mg sod., 37g carb. (10g sugars, 8g fiber), 11g pro.

⑤ⓘ SOUR CREAM CUCUMBERS

It's been a tradition at our house to serve this dish with the other Hungarian specialties my mom learned to make from the women at church. It's especially good during the summer when the cucumbers are fresh-picked from the garden.
—*Pamela Eaton, Monclova, OH*

PREP: 15 MIN. + CHILLING • **MAKES:** 8 SERVINGS

½ cup sour cream
3 Tbsp. white vinegar
1 Tbsp. sugar
 Pepper to taste
4 medium cucumbers, peeled, if desired, and thinly sliced
1 small sweet onion, thinly sliced and separated into rings

In a large bowl, whisk sour cream, vinegar, sugar and pepper until blended. Add cucumbers and onion; toss to coat. Refrigerate, covered, for at least 4 hours. Serve with a slotted spoon.

¾ CUP 62 cal., 3g fat (2g sat. fat), 10mg chol., 5mg sod., 7g carb. (5g sugars, 2g fiber), 2g pro. **DIABETIC EXCHANGES** 1 vegetable, ½ fat.

CUCUMBERS WITH DILL Omit first 4 ingredients. Mix ¾ cup white vinegar, ⅓ cup snipped fresh dill, ⅓ cup sugar and ¾ tsp. pepper. Stir in cucumbers and onion.

TEST KITCHEN TIP

Many grocery store cucumbers are coated with protective wax to prolong freshness. They should be peeled before eating. There's no need to peel English cucumbers that are wrapped in plastic. Ditto for cukes from the farmers market or your own garden. Whether or not to peel these is a taste preference.

❄ SWEET ONION SPOON BREAD

This unique recipe has been a family favorite for years. The layers of tangy cheese, sour cream and sweet onions in the moist cornbread taste so amazing together. Add chopped green chiles for extra zip.

—Heather Thomas, Fredericksburg, VA

PREP: 15 MIN. • **BAKE:** 25 MIN. • **MAKES:** 9 SERVINGS

1⅓ cups chopped sweet onions
1 Tbsp. butter
1 can (8¼ oz.) cream-style corn
1 pkg. (8½ oz.) cornbread/muffin mix
2 large egg whites, lightly beaten
2 Tbsp. fat-free milk
½ cup reduced-fat sour cream
⅓ cup shredded sharp cheddar cheese

1. In a small nonstick skillet, saute onions in butter until tender; set aside.

2. Meanwhile, in a large bowl, combine corn, muffin mix, egg whites and milk. Pour into a 9-in. square baking dish coated with cooking spray. Combine sour cream and onions; spread over batter. Sprinkle with cheese.

3. Bake, uncovered, at 350° until a toothpick inserted in center comes out clean, 25-30 minutes.

1 PIECE 191 cal., 6g fat (3g sat. fat), 18mg chol., 361mg sod., 29g carb. (10g sugars, 1g fiber), 6g pro. **DIABETIC EXCHANGES** 2 starch, ½ fat.

TEST KITCHEN TIP

Sweet onions are easy to recognize by their shape. They are shorter from pole to pole and bigger around than regular cooking onions. Many carry the names from the place they're grown, such as Vidalia (from Vidalia, Georgia), Walla Walla (from Washington) and the Maui onion from Hawaii.

(5i) BLACK-EYED PEAS WITH HAM

Here's a regional favorite I grew to love after moving to the South. Serve the dish as a side with grilled chicken, or make it your main course and round out the meal with greens and cornbread.
—*Tammie Merrill, Wake Forest, NC*

PREP: 10 MIN. + SOAKING • **COOK:** 8 HOURS • **MAKES:** 10 SERVINGS

1 pkg. (16 oz.) dried
  black-eyed peas
1 cup cubed fully cooked
  ham
1 medium onion,
  finely chopped
3 garlic cloves, minced
2 tsp. seasoned salt
1 tsp. pepper
4 cups water
  Thinly sliced green onions,
  optional

Rinse and sort black-eyed peas; soak according to package directions. Drain and rinse peas, discarding liquid. Transfer peas to a 4-qt. slow cooker. Stir in next 6 ingredients. Cook, covered, on low 8-10 hours or until peas are tender. Serve with a slotted spoon. Sprinkle with green onions if desired.
¾ CUP 76 cal., 1g fat (0 sat. fat), 8mg chol., 476mg sod., 11g carb. (2g sugars, 3g fiber), 7g pro.

(5i) CARROT RAISIN SALAD

This traditional salad is one of my mother-in-law's favorites. It's fun to eat because of the crunchy texture, and the raisins give it a slightly sweet flavor. Plus, I love how easy it is to make.
—*Denise Baumert, Dalhart, TX*

TAKES: 10 MIN. • **MAKES:** 8 SERVINGS

4 cups shredded carrots
¾ to 1½ cups raisins
¼ cup mayonnaise
2 Tbsp. sugar
2 to 3 Tbsp. 2% milk

Mix the first 4 ingredients. Stir in enough milk to reach desired consistency. Refrigerate until serving.
½ CUP 122 cal., 5g fat (1g sat. fat), 1mg chol., 76mg sod., 19g carb. (14g sugars, 2g fiber), 1g pro. **DIABETIC EXCHANGES** 1 vegetable, 1 fat, ½ starch, ½ fruit.

BLACK-EYED
PEAS WITH HAM

PEPPERONI ANGEL HAIR

This noodle side dish is so versatile that it can accompany steak, pork chops, chicken or even hamburgers. Chill leftovers to serve as a cool main-dish salad on a warm summer night. When time allows, I like to replace the pepperoni with sliced cooked chicken.

—*Julie Mosher, Coldwater, MI*

TAKES: 10 MIN. • **MAKES:** 10 SERVINGS

- 8 oz. uncooked angel hair pasta, broken into thirds
- 1 small cucumber, peeled and chopped
- 1 medium green pepper, chopped
- 1 pkg. (8 oz.) sliced pepperoni, quartered
- 2 cans (2¼ oz. each) sliced ripe olives, drained
- ½ cup Italian salad dressing
- 1¼ cups shredded Parmesan cheese

Cook pasta according to package directions. Meanwhile, combine cucumber, green pepper, pepperoni and olives in a large bowl. Drain pasta and rinse in cold water; add to pepperoni mixture. Drizzle with salad dressing and sprinkle with Parmesan cheese; toss to coat.

1 SERVING 483 cal., 31g fat (11g sat. fat), 44mg chol., 1413mg sod., 33g carb. (4g sugars, 2g fiber), 19g pro.

READER REVIEW

"Yum! Easy to cater to your liking. We added halved grape tomatoes and omitted the olives. We didn't bother peeling the cucumber either. It's great with turkey pepperoni and thin whole wheat spaghetti."
—LURKY27, TASTEOFHOME.COM

❄ FAVORITE CHEESY POTATOES

My family loves these potatoes. I make a large batch in disposable pans and serve them at all our get-togethers. The holidays aren't the same without them. It's also a wonderful recipe for Christmas morning brunch.

—*Brenda Smith, Curran, MI*

PREP: 30 MIN. • **BAKE:** 45 MIN. • **MAKES:** 12 SERVINGS

3½ **lbs. potatoes (about 7 medium), peeled and cut into ¾-in. cubes**
1 **can (10½ oz.) condensed cream of potato soup, undiluted**
1 **cup French onion dip**
¾ **cup 2% milk**
⅔ **cup sour cream**
1 **tsp. minced fresh parsley**
¼ **tsp. salt**
¼ **tsp. pepper**
1 **pkg. (16 oz.) Velveeta, cubed**
Additional minced fresh parsley

1. Preheat oven to 350°. Place potatoes in a Dutch oven; add water to cover. Bring to a boil. Reduce heat; cook, uncovered, until potatoes are tender, 8-12 minutes. Drain. Cool slightly.

2. In a large bowl, mix soup, onion dip, milk, sour cream, parsley, salt and pepper; gently fold in potatoes and cheese. Transfer to a greased 13x9-in. baking dish.

3. Bake, covered, 30 minutes. Uncover; bake until heated through and cheese is melted, 15-20 minutes longer. Just before serving, stir to combine; sprinkle with fresh parsley. (Potatoes will thicken upon standing.)

FREEZE OPTION Cover and freeze unbaked casserole. To use, partially thaw in refrigerator overnight. Remove from refrigerator 30 minutes before baking. Preheat oven to 350°. Cover casserole with foil; bake 1¼-1½ hours or until heated through and a thermometer inserted in center reads 165°. Uncover; bake until lightly browned, 15-20 minutes longer. Just before serving, stir to combine. If desired, sprinkle with additional parsley.

½ CUP 294 cal., 16g fat (10g sat. fat), 42mg chol., 813mg sod., 26g carb. (6g sugars, 2g fiber), 10g pro.

51 PRESSURE-COOKER GREEN BEANS

Free up room on your stovetop when you're cooking for company, and make this easy green bean recipe in a pressure cooker. Mix and match with your favorite herbs and spices. It really does take only 1 minute to get crisp-tender green beans.
—*Peggy Woodward, Shullsburg, WI*

PREP: 10 MIN. • **COOK:** 5 MIN. • **MAKES:** 10 SERVINGS

2 lbs. fresh green beans, trimmed
¼ cup chopped fresh parsley
3 Tbsp. butter, melted
2 Tbsp. minced chives
2 Tbsp. lemon juice
1 tsp. salt
¼ tsp. pepper
Chopped toasted walnuts, optional

1. Place steamer basket and 1 cup water in a 6-qt. electric pressure cooker. Set green beans in basket. Lock lid; close pressure-release valve. Adjust to pressure-cook on high for 1 minute. Quick-release pressure; drain.

2. Return beans to pressure cooker. Add parsley, butter, chives, lemon juice, salt and pepper; toss to coat. If desired, sprinkle with nuts.

¾ CUP 60 cal., 4g fat (2g sat. fat), 9mg chol., 270mg sod., 7g carb. (2g sugars, 3g fiber), 2g pro. **DIABETIC EXCHANGES** 1 vegetable, 1 fat.

EASY DOES IT

Fresh green beans are available year-round and should be easy to find at your local grocery store. In case they aren't available, frozen green beans work as a great alternative, even more so than canned ones.

⑤ PISTACHIO MALLOW SALAD

This fluffy salad is a real treat since it's creamy but not overly sweet. It's easy to mix up, and the flavor gets better the longer it stands. It's perfect for St. Patrick's Day, served in a green bowl.
—*Pattie Ann Forssberg, Logan, KS*

PREP: 10 MIN. + CHILLING • **MAKES:** 12 SERVINGS

1 carton (16 oz.) whipped topping
1 pkg. (3.4 oz.) instant pistachio pudding mix
6 to 7 drops green food coloring, optional
3 cups miniature marshmallows
1 can (20 oz.) pineapple tidbits, undrained
½ cup chopped pistachios or walnuts
Additional whipped topping, optional

In a large bowl, combine whipped topping, pudding mix and, if desired, food coloring. Fold in marshmallows and pineapple. Cover and refrigerate for at least 2 hours. Just before serving, top with additional whipped topping if desired, and sprinkle with nuts.

¾ CUP 236 cal., 9g fat (7g sat. fat), 0 chol., 140mg sod., 35g carb. (23g sugars, 1g fiber), 2g pro.

TEST KITCHEN TIP

Consider serving the pistachio salad as a side dish to sliced glazed ham for a delicious spring meal and with leftover ham sandwiches the next day. It also goes well with most main dishes you'd find at a potluck or barbecue.

ITALIAN-STYLE
CRESCENTS, PAGE 79

LAZY-DAY
BREADS

BAKING POWDER DROP BISCUITS

One day I had company coming and realized I had run out of biscuit mix. I'd never made biscuits from scratch before, but I decided to give this recipe a try. Now this is the only way I make them!
—*Sharon Evans, Clear Lake, IA*

TAKES: 20 MIN. • **MAKES:** 1 DOZEN

2 cups all-purpose flour
2 Tbsp. sugar
4 tsp. baking powder
½ tsp. cream of tartar
½ tsp. salt
½ cup shortening
⅔ cup 2% milk
1 large egg, room temperature

1. Preheat oven to 450°. In a large bowl, combine the first 5 ingredients. Cut in shortening until the mixture resembles coarse crumbs. In a small bowl, whisk the milk and egg. Stir into crumb mixture just until moistened.
2. Drop by ¼ cupfuls 2 in. apart onto an ungreased baking sheet. Bake until golden brown, 10-12 minutes. Serve warm.
1 BISCUIT 170 cal., 9g fat (2g sat. fat), 17mg chol., 271mg sod., 19g carb. (3g sugars, 1g fiber), 3g pro.

⑤ⓘ HONEY BEER BREAD

It's true—this yummy bread requires only four ingredients! Simply combine self-rising flour, sugar, honey and beer, pour the batter into the pan and bake.
—*Cak Marshall, Salem, OR*

PREP: 5 MIN. • **BAKE:** 45 MIN. + COOLING
MAKES: 1 LOAF (12 PIECES)

3 cups self-rising flour
3 Tbsp. sugar
⅓ cup honey
1 bottle (12 oz.) beer

1. Preheat oven to 350°. In a large bowl, whisk flour and sugar. Stir in honey and beer just until moistened.
2. Transfer to a greased 8x4-in. loaf pan. Bake 45-50 minutes or until a toothpick inserted in center comes out clean. Cool in pan 10 minutes before removing to a wire rack to cool.
1 PIECE 163 cal., 0 fat (0 sat. fat), 0 chol., 374mg sod., 35g carb. (12g sugars, 1g fiber), 3g pro.

BAKING POWDER
DROP BISCUITS

⑤ ❄ EASY BATTER ROLLS

The first thing my guests ask when they come for dinner is if I'm serving these dinner rolls. The buns are so light, airy and delicious that I'm constantly asked for the recipe.
—*Thomasina Brunner, Gloversville, NY*

PREP: 30 MIN. + RISING • **BAKE:** 15 MIN. • **MAKES:** 1 DOZEN

3 cups all-purpose flour
2 Tbsp. sugar
1 pkg. (¼ oz.) active dry yeast
1 tsp. salt
1 cup water
2 Tbsp. butter
1 large egg, room
   temperature
   Melted butter

1. In a large mixer bowl, combine 2 cups flour, sugar, yeast and salt. In a saucepan, heat water and butter to 120°-130°. Add to dry ingredients; beat until blended. Add egg; beat on low speed for 30 seconds, then on high for 3 minutes. Stir in enough of the remaining flour to form a stiff dough. Do not knead. Cover and let rise in a warm place until doubled, about 30 minutes.

2. Stir dough down. Fill 12 greased muffin cups half full. Cover and let rise until doubled, about 15 minutes.

3. Bake at 350° until golden brown, 15-20 minutes. Cool for 1 minute before removing from pan to a wire rack. Brush tops with melted butter.

FREEZE OPTION Freeze cooled rolls in airtight containers. To use, microwave each roll on high until warmed, 30-45 seconds.

1 ROLL 147 cal., 3g fat (1g sat. fat), 21mg chol., 219mg sod., 26g carb. (2g sugars, 1g fiber), 4g pro.

READER REVIEW
"Such good, fast rolls! Despite the quick rise time, they are still soft and fluffy and not tough at all! Definitely making these again!"
—HKAROW1793, TASTEOFHOME.COM

❋ PECAN RAISIN BREAD

We love raisin bread and also enjoy the nutty flavor of pecans, so I decided to combine the two for this delectable loaf. It smells terrific and tastes so good!
—*Lora Sexton, Wellington, TX*

PREP: 10 MIN. • **BAKE:** 3 HOURS • **MAKES:** 1 LOAF (2½ LBS., 16 SLICES)

1 cup plus 2 Tbsp. water (70° to 80°)
8 tsp. butter
1 large egg, room temperature
6 Tbsp. sugar
¼ cup nonfat dry milk powder
1 tsp. salt
4 cups bread flour
1 Tbsp. active dry yeast
1 cup finely chopped pecans
1 cup raisins

1. In bread machine pan, place the first 8 ingredients in order suggested by manufacturer. Select basic bread setting. Choose crust color and loaf size if available.

2. Bake according to bread machine directions (check dough after 5 minutes of mixing; add 1-2 Tbsp. water or flour if needed).

3. Just before the final kneading (your machine may audibly signal this), add pecans and raisins.

FREEZE OPTION Securely wrap and freeze cooled loaf in foil and place in resealable plastic freezer bag. To use, thaw at room temperature.

NOTE We recommend you do not use a bread machine's time-delay feature for this recipe.

1 PIECE 227 cal., 8g fat (2g sat. fat), 19mg chol., 182mg sod., 36g carb. (12g sugars, 2g fiber), 6g pro.

SLOW-COOKER MONKEY BREAD

I often take this monkey bread to church potlucks—children and adults alike love it! The rum extract is optional.

—*Lisa Leaper, Worthington, OH*

PREP: 20 MIN. • **COOK:** 2½ HOURS + STANDING • **MAKES:** 10 SERVINGS

1 cup sugar
¾ cup packed brown sugar
2 tsp. ground cinnamon
½ tsp. ground allspice
4 tubes (6 oz. each) refrigerated buttermilk biscuits
¾ cup butter, melted
½ cup apple juice
1 tsp. vanilla extract
1 tsp. rum extract
Toasted chopped pecans, optional

1. Line a 5-qt. slow cooker with a piece of aluminum foil, letting ends extend up the sides. Grease foil.

2. Combine sugars, cinnamon and allspice in a large bowl; sprinkle 3 Tbsp. sugar mixture in bottom of prepared slow cooker. Cut biscuits in quarters. Add biscuit pieces to bowl; toss to coat. Transfer coated biscuits to slow cooker; sprinkle any remaining sugar mixture over biscuits.

3. Stir together butter, apple juice and extracts; pour over biscuits.

4. Cook, covered, on low 2½-3 hours. Remove lid and let stand for 10 minutes. Carefully invert onto a serving platter. If desired, sprinkle with pecans.

8 BISCUIT PIECES 473 cal., 22g fat (12g sat. fat), 37mg chol., 675mg sod., 68g carb. (41g sugars, 0 fiber), 4g pro.

TEST KITCHEN TIP

Dark brown sugar contains more molasses than light or golden brown sugar. The types are generally interchangeable in recipes. But if you prefer a bolder flavor, choose dark brown sugar.

FROSTED PUMPKIN MUFFINS

These easy pumpkin muffins with cake mix are so good, even picky eaters cannot seem to get enough. They're also delicious without frosting or nuts.
—*Samantha Callahan, Muncie, IN*

PREP: 20 MIN. • **BAKE:** 20 MIN. • **MAKES:** 1½ DOZEN

1 **pkg. (16 oz.) lb. cake mix**
1 **cup canned pumpkin**
2 **large eggs, room temperature**
⅓ **cup water**
2 **tsp. pumpkin pie spice**
1 **tsp. baking soda**
1 **can (16 oz.) cream cheese frosting**
½ **cup finely chopped pecans, optional**

1. In a large bowl, combine the cake mix, pumpkin, eggs, water, pumpkin pie spice and baking soda; beat on low speed for 30 seconds. Scrape side and bottom of bowl. Beat on medium for 2 minutes.

2. Fill 18 greased or paper-lined muffin cups two-thirds full. Bake at 350° until a toothpick comes out clean, 18-22 minutes. Cool 5 minutes before removing from pans to wire racks to cool completely.

3. Frost muffins. Sprinkle with pecans if desired. Store in the refrigerator.

1 MUFFIN 217 cal., 6g fat (3g sat. fat), 21mg chol., 220mg sod., 40g carb. (27g sugars, 1g fiber), 2g pro.

TEST KITCHEN TIPS

- Fold chocolate chips into the batter if desired.

- You can make mini pumpkin muffins with this recipe. Fill mini muffin cups ⅔ full with batter and bake until a toothpick comes out clean, 12-16 minutes.

ITALIAN-STYLE
CRESCENTS

5i ITALIAN-STYLE CRESCENTS

This is one of my best easy breads. Pesto and Italian seasoning are a quick upgrade for refrigerated crescent roll dough.
—*Ann Marie Barber, Oakland Park, FL*

TAKES: 25 MIN. • **MAKES:** 8 SERVINGS

- 1 tube (8 oz.) refrigerated crescent rolls
- 8 tsp. prepared pesto
- 1 large egg white, lightly beaten
- 1½ tsp. Italian seasoning

1. Preheat oven to 375°. Unroll dough; separate into triangles. Spread each with 1 tsp. pesto. Roll up from wide end and place pointed side down 2 in. apart on ungreased baking sheets. Gently curve ends down to form a crescent shape.
2. Brush with egg white; sprinkle with Italian seasoning. Bake until lightly browned, 10-13 minutes.

1 CROISSANT 140 cal., 8g fat (2g sat. fat), 2mg chol., 269mg sod., 12g carb. (2g sugars, 0 fiber), 3g pro.

BLUE CHEESE GARLIC BREAD

This is an irresistible way to dress up an ordinary loaf of bread. Serve slices as an appetizer or with a meal.
—*Kevalyn Henderson, Hayward, WI*

TAKES: 30 MIN. • **MAKES:** 10 SERVINGS

- ½ cup butter, softened
- 4 oz. crumbled blue cheese
- 2 Tbsp. grated Parmesan cheese
- 1 Tbsp. minced chives
- 1 tsp. garlic powder
- 1 loaf (1 lb.) unsliced French bread

1. In a small bowl, combine the first 5 ingredients. Cut into bread to make 1-in.-thick slices, but don't cut all the way through—leave slices attached at the bottom. Spread cheese mixture between the slices.
2. Wrap loaf in a large piece of heavy-duty foil (about 28x18 in.); fold around bread and seal tightly. Bake at 350° until heated through, about 20 minutes. Serve warm.

1 PIECE 250 cal., 14g fat (8g sat. fat), 34mg chol., 546mg sod., 24g carb. (1g sugars, 1g fiber), 7g pro.

⑤ⓘ SLOW-COOKER BANANA BREAD

I love to use my slow cooker. I started to experiment with making bread in it so I wouldn't have to heat up my kitchen by turning on my oven. It's so easy and simple. I now make it this way all the time.
—*Nicole Gackowski, Antioch, CA*

PREP: 10 MIN. • **COOK:** 2½ HOURS • **MAKES:** 16 SERVINGS

5   medium ripe bananas
2½ cups self-rising flour
1   can (14 oz.) sweetened
    condensed milk
1   tsp. ground cinnamon
    Cinnamon sugar, optional

1. Place a piece of parchment in a 5-qt. slow cooker, letting ends extend up the side. Grease paper with cooking spray. Combine the first 4 ingredients in a large bowl. Pour batter into prepared slow cooker. If desired, sprinkle cinnamon sugar over the top of batter. Cover slow cooker with a double layer of white paper towels; place lid securely over towels.

2. Cook, covered, on high until the bread is lightly browned, 2½-3 hours. To avoid scorching, rotate slow cooker insert a half turn midway through cooking, lifting carefully with oven mitts. Using the parchment to lift, remove bread from the slow cooker; let cool slightly before slicing.

NOTE As a substitute for each cup of self-rising flour, place 1½ tsp. baking powder and ½ tsp. salt in a measuring cup. Add all-purpose flour to measure 1 cup.

1 PIECE 210 cal., 3g fat (2g sat. fat), 11mg chol., 276mg sod., 41g carb. (23g sugars, 2g fiber), 5g pro.

SALLY LUNN BATTER BREAD

The tantalizing aroma of this golden loaf baking in the oven always draws people into my mother's kitchen. With its circular shape, it's a pretty bread too. I've never seen it last more than two days!

—*Jeanne Voss, Anaheim Hills, CA*

PREP: 15 MIN. + RISING • **BAKE:** 25 MIN. • **MAKES:** 16 SERVINGS

1 pkg. (¼ oz.) active dry yeast
½ cup warm water (110° to 115°)
1 cup warm 2% milk (110° to 115°)
½ cup butter, softened
¼ cup sugar
2 tsp. salt
3 large eggs, room temperature
5½ to 6 cups all-purpose flour

HONEY BUTTER
½ cup butter, softened
½ cup honey

1. In a large bowl, dissolve yeast in warm water. Add milk, butter, sugar, salt, eggs and 3 cups flour; beat until smooth. Stir in enough remaining flour to form a soft dough.

2. Do not knead. Place in a greased bowl, turning once to grease the top. Cover and let rise in a warm place until doubled, about 1 hour.

3. Stir the dough down. Spoon into a greased and floured 10-in. tube pan. Cover and let rise until doubled, about 1 hour.

4. Bake at 400° for 25-30 minutes or until golden brown. Remove from pan to a wire rack to cool.

5. Combine the honey butter ingredients until smooth. Serve with bread.

1 PIECE 326 cal., 13g fat (8g sat. fat), 73mg chol., 431mg sod., 46g carb. (13g sugars, 1g fiber), 6g pro.

5i QUICK FOCACCIA

Green olives complement my speedy version of the beloved Italian bread. Try the focaccia with minestrone or Italian wedding soup, or serve it with an antipasto tray for a hearty appetizer everyone will love.
—Ivy Laffoon, Ceres, CA

TAKES: 30 MIN. • **MAKES:** 8 SERVINGS

- 1 loaf (1 lb.) frozen bread dough, thawed
- ½ cup sliced pimiento-stuffed olives
- ½ cup shredded Colby-Monterey Jack cheese
- ½ cup shredded Parmesan cheese
- 1 tsp. Italian seasoning
- 2 Tbsp. olive oil

1. On an ungreased baking sheet, pat the dough into a 12x6-in. rectangle. Build up edges slightly. Top with the olives, cheeses and Italian seasoning; press gently into dough. Drizzle with oil.
2. Bake at 350° until cheese is melted and golden brown, 15-20 minutes. Let stand for 5 minutes before slicing.
1 PIECE 249 cal., 11g fat (3g sat. fat), 10mg chol., 623mg sod., 31g carb. (2g sugars, 2g fiber), 9g pro.

5i SMALL BATCH POPOVERS

These golden popovers are a wonderful way to round out any meal. My husband and I have enjoyed these popovers often during our 50 years together.
—Pauline Sniezek, Adams, MA

TAKES: 25 MIN. • **MAKES:** 4 POPOVERS

- ½ cup all-purpose flour
- ¼ tsp. salt
- 2 large eggs, room temperature
- ½ cup milk

In a small bowl, combine flour and salt. Whisk together eggs and milk; stir into dry ingredients just until blended. Pour into 4 greased and floured 8-oz. custard cups. Place on a baking sheet. Bake, uncovered, at 425° for 20 minutes or until puffed and edges are golden brown (do not open oven door during baking).
2 POPOVERS 226 cal., 7g fat (3g sat. fat), 221mg chol., 389mg sod., 27g carb. (4g sugars, 1g fiber), 11g pro.

QUICK
FOCACCIA

5i NO-KNEAD, NO-ROLL, NO-CUT BISCUITS

As a Southerner and our household cook, I experimented until I hit on just the right biscuit recipe. It practically screams to be smothered in gravy or stuffed with eggs and sausage.
—*Susan Flippin, Mt. Airy, NC*

TAKES: 30 MIN. • **MAKES:** 8 BISCUITS

2⅓ cups self-rising flour, divided
¼ cup cold butter or shortening
¾ to 1 cup 2% milk
2 Tbsp. butter, melted

1. Preheat oven to 375°. Place 2 cups flour in a large bowl. Cut in butter until mixture is the size of peas. Stir in ¾ cup milk. Dough should be sticky; if needed, stir in some of the remaining milk.

2. Place remaining flour in a small bowl. Using a ¼-cup measuring cup dipped in flour, remove a scant ¼ cup dough from bowl and drop into flour; gently turn to coat. Place in greased cast-iron or other ovenproof pan. Repeat with remaining dough.

3. Bake until golden brown, 20-25 minutes. Brush with melted butter; serve warm.

1 BISCUIT 217 cal., 9g fat (6g sat. fat), 25mg chol., 514mg sod., 28g carb. (1g sugars, 1g fiber), 4g pro.

TEST KITCHEN TIP

To keep biscuits at room temperature, wrap them tightly in foil, then store in an airtight container for 1-2 days. You can store them in the fridge for up to a week—this is ideal if you've mixed in perishable ingredients such as cheese. For long-term tenderness, freeze them by wrapping them and storing in an airtight container. They will last 1-2 months.

SLOW-COOKED
CORN CHOWDER,
PAGE 122

LAZY-DAY
SOUPS

EFFORTLESS BLACK BEAN CHILI

My mom found the inspiration for this chili in a slow-cooker cookbook. After a few updates, we all love it (even those of us who steer clear of beans). We think it's even better served over rice.
—Amelia Gormley, Ephrata, PA

PREP: 25 MIN. • **COOK:** 6 HOURS • **MAKES:** 6 SERVINGS

1 lb. ground turkey
1 small onion, chopped
3 tsp. chili powder
2 tsp. minced fresh oregano or ¾ tsp. dried oregano
1 tsp. chicken bouillon granules
1 jar (16 oz.) mild salsa
1 can (15¼ oz.) whole kernel corn, drained
1 can (15 oz.) black beans, rinsed and drained
1 can (14½ oz.) diced tomatoes, undrained
½ cup water
Optional toppings: Sour cream, finely chopped red onion, chopped cilantro and corn chips

1. In a large skillet, cook and crumble turkey with onion over medium-high heat until no longer pink, 5-7 minutes. Transfer to a 4-qt. slow cooker.

2. Stir in all remaining ingredients except toppings. Cook, covered, on low until flavors are blended, 6-8 hours. Top as desired.

1 CUP 242 cal., 6g fat (1g sat. fat), 50mg chol., 868mg sod., 26g carb. (9g sugars, 6g fiber), 20g pro.

TEST KITCHEN TIPS

• We used thick and chunky salsa for more texture.

• If you prefer, use about 1¾ cups frozen corn instead of canned.

QUICK SAUSAGE TORTELLINI SOUP

I love that this soup is easy to make and uses common ingredients found in the pantry. You can use other types of sausage or pasta if desired.
—*Annalise Lau, Newberg, OR*

PREP: 20 MIN. • **COOK:** 15 MIN. • **MAKES:** 8 SERVINGS (3 QT.)

3 Italian turkey sausage links, casings removed
1 medium onion, chopped
4 garlic cloves, minced
¼ tsp. crushed red pepper flakes
6 cups reduced-sodium chicken broth
1 jar (24 oz.) pasta sauce
1 can (15 oz.) crushed tomatoes
2 Tbsp. tomato paste
2 tsp. dried basil
2 tsp. balsamic vinegar
1 tsp. dried parsley flakes
1½ tsp. sugar
½ tsp. dried oregano
¼ tsp. salt
½ tsp. pepper
2 cups frozen cheese tortellini
Shredded Parmesan cheese, optional

1. In a Dutch oven, cook sausage and onion over medium heat until sausage is no longer pink and onion is tender, 5-7 minutes, breaking up sausage into crumbles; drain. Add the garlic and pepper flakes; cook 1 minute longer. Stir in the broth, pasta sauce, crushed tomatoes, tomato paste, basil, vinegar, parsley flakes, sugar, oregano, salt and pepper; bring to a boil.

2. Add tortellini; cook, uncovered, until tortellini are tender, 3-5 minutes, stirring occasionally. Serve immediately. If desired, top with cheese.

1½ CUPS 192 cal., 5g fat (1g sat. fat), 24mg chol., 1167mg sod., 26g carb. (12g sugars, 4g fiber), 12g pro.

READER REVIEW
"This was good! I made it tonight, just as written, except I sprinkled Asiago cheese on it at the end instead of Parmesan. The flavors are wonderful. And it's quick and easy! I'll make this again for sure."
—DMKINSEY, TASTEOFHOME.COM

❄ MINESTRONE WITH TURKEY

I remember my mom making this soup; now I make it as often as I can. It's a good way to use up leftover vegetables. Sometimes I add a can of rinsed and drained kidney or garbanzo beans.
—*Angela Goodman, Kaneohe, HI*

TAKES: 30 MIN. • **MAKES:** 6 SERVINGS (ABOUT 2 QT.)

1 Tbsp. olive oil
1 medium onion, chopped
1 medium carrot, sliced
1 celery rib, sliced
1 garlic clove, minced
4 cups chicken broth or homemade turkey stock
1 can (14½ oz.) diced tomatoes, undrained
⅔ cup each frozen peas, corn and cut green beans, thawed
½ cup uncooked elbow macaroni
1 tsp. salt
¼ tsp. dried basil
¼ tsp. dried oregano
¼ tsp. pepper
1 bay leaf
1 cup cubed cooked turkey
1 small zucchini, halved lengthwise and cut into ¼-in. slices
¼ cup grated Parmesan cheese, optional

1. In a Dutch oven, heat oil over medium-high heat. Add onion, carrot and celery; cook and stir until tender. Add garlic; cook 1 minute longer. Add broth, tomatoes, vegetables, macaroni and seasonings. Bring to a boil. Reduce the heat; simmer, uncovered, 5 minutes or until macaroni is al dente.

2. Stir in turkey and zucchini; cook until zucchini is crisp-tender. Discard bay leaf. If desired, sprinkle servings with cheese.

FREEZE OPTION Transfer cooled soup to freezer container and freeze up to 3 months. To use, thaw in the refrigerator overnight. Transfer to a saucepan. Cover and cook over medium heat until heated through. Serve with cheese if desired.

1¼ CUPS 172 cal., 5g fat (1g sat. fat), 24mg chol., 1251mg sod., 20g carb. (7g sugars, 4g fiber), 12g pro.

READER REVIEW
"I used some leftover turkey to make this delicious soup. I followed the recipe exactly except I used about 1½ cups turkey instead of just 1 cup. Next time I make it, I think I'll add some rinsed and drained kidney beans or garbanzo beans too. This is a wonderful brothy soup .... five stars!"
—BICKTASW, TASTEOFHOME.COM

CHEESE
CHICKEN SOUP

5i CHEESE CHICKEN SOUP

Kids won't think twice about eating vegetables once they're incorporated into this creamy and cheesy soup.
—*LaVonne Lundgren, Sioux City, IA*

TAKES: 30 MIN. • **MAKES:** 8 SERVINGS (2⅔ QT.)

4 cups shredded cooked chicken breast
3½ cups water
2 cans (10¾ oz. each) condensed cream of chicken soup, undiluted
1 pkg. (16 oz.) frozen mixed vegetables, thawed
1 can (14½ oz.) diced potatoes, drained
1 lb. Velveeta, cubed
Minced chives, optional

1. In a Dutch oven, combine chicken, water, condensed soup, frozen vegetables and potatoes. Bring to a boil. Reduce heat; cover and simmer until vegetables are tender, 8-10 minutes.

2. Stir in cheese just until melted (do not boil). If desired, top with minced fresh chives.

1⅓ CUPS 429 cal., 22g fat (11g sat. fat), 116mg chol., 1464mg sod., 23g carb. (6g sugars, 4g fiber), 33g pro.

SPEEDY CREAM OF WILD RICE SOUP

Add homemade touches to a can of potato soup to get comfort food on the table quickly. The result is a thick and creamy treat textured with wild rice and flavored with smoky bacon.
—*Joanne Eickhoff, Pequot Lakes, MN*

TAKES: 20 MIN. • **MAKES:** 2 SERVINGS

½ cup water
4½ tsp. dried minced onion
⅔ cup condensed cream of potato soup, undiluted
½ cup shredded Swiss cheese
½ cup cooked wild rice
½ cup half-and-half cream
2 bacon strips, cooked and crumbled

In a small saucepan, bring water and onion to a boil. Reduce heat. Stir in potato soup, cheese, wild rice and half-and-half cream; heat through (do not boil). Garnish each serving with bacon.

1 CUP 333 cal., 18g fat (11g sat. fat), 68mg chol., 835mg sod., 24g carb. (5g sugars, 2g fiber), 15g pro.

SLOW-COOKED MEXICAN BEEF SOUP

My family loves this soup, and I'm happy to make it since it's so simple! You can serve it with cornbread instead of corn chips to make it an even more filling meal.

—Angela Lively, Conroe, TX

PREP: 15 MIN. • **COOK:** 6 HOURS • **MAKES:** 6 SERVINGS (2 QT.)

1 lb. beef stew meat (1¼-in. pieces)

¾ lb. potatoes (about 2 medium), cut into ¾-in. cubes

2 cups frozen corn (about 10 oz.), thawed

2 medium carrots, cut into ½-in. slices

1 medium onion, chopped

2 garlic cloves, minced

1½ tsp. dried oregano

1 tsp. ground cumin

½ tsp. salt

¼ tsp. crushed red pepper flakes

2 cups beef stock

1 can (10 oz.) diced tomatoes and green chiles, undrained

Optional toppings: Sour cream and tortilla chips

In a 5- or 6-qt. slow cooker, combine first 12 ingredients. Cook, covered, on low until meat is tender, 6-8 hours. If desired, serve with sour cream and chips.

1⅓ CUPS 218 cal., 6g fat (2g sat. fat), 47mg chol., 602mg sod., 24g carb. (5g sugars, 3g fiber), 19g pro. **DIABETIC EXCHANGES** 2 lean meat, 1½ starch.

PRESSURE-COOKER POTATO SOUP

I decided to add some character to a basic potato chowder with roasted red peppers. The extra flavor gives a deliciously unique twist to an otherwise ordinary soup.
—*Mary Shivers, Ada, OK*

PREP: 20 MIN. • **COOK:** 25 MIN. • **MAKES:** 12 SERVINGS (3 QT.)

3   lbs. potatoes, peeled and cut into ½-in. cubes (about 8 cups)
1   large onion, chopped
1   jar (7 oz.) roasted sweet red peppers, drained and chopped
1   small celery rib, chopped
6   cups chicken broth
½   tsp. garlic powder
½   tsp. seasoned salt
½   tsp. pepper
⅛   tsp. rubbed sage
⅓   cup all-purpose flour
2   cups heavy whipping cream, divided
1   cup grated Parmesan cheese, divided
8   bacon strips, cooked and crumbled
2   Tbsp. minced fresh cilantro

1. Place first 9 ingredients in a 6-qt. electric pressure cooker. Lock lid; close pressure-release valve. Adjust pressure to pressure-cook on high for 15 minutes. Quick-release pressure.
2. Select saute setting and adjust for low heat. Mix flour and ½ cup cream until smooth; stir into the soup. Stir in ¾ cup Parmesan cheese, bacon, cilantro and remaining 1½ cups cream. Cook and stir until slightly thickened, 6-8 minutes. Serve with remaining ¼ cup cheese.
1 CUP 289 cal., 19g fat (11g sat. fat), 59mg chol., 848mg sod., 23g carb. (4g sugars, 1g fiber), 7g pro.

EASY DOES IT

Any combination of potatoes will work in this recipe, but russet potatoes hold up best to the heat.

QUICK WHITE CHILI

This recipe went from a gigantic mistake to a tasty triumph. I created it by accident—and it got rave reviews. Now I whip up this quick-as-lightning dish when I'm pinched for time.
—*Cynthia Lynn Bloemker, Effingham, IL*

TAKES: 10 MIN. • **MAKES:** 8 SERVINGS (2 QT.)

1 jar (48 oz.) great northern beans, rinsed and drained
2 cans (one 10 oz., one 5 oz.) chunk white chicken, drained
1¼ cups whole milk
1 cup sour cream
1 can (4 oz.) chopped green chiles
1 tsp. salt-free seasoning blend
1 cup shredded Italian cheese blend
2 Tbsp. minced fresh cilantro
Optional toppings: Additional sour cream and minced fresh cilantro

In a large saucepan, combine the first 6 ingredients. Bring to a boil over medium-high heat; remove from the heat. Add cheese and cilantro; stir until cheese is melted. If desired, serve with additional sour cream and cilantro.

1 CUP 310 cal., 11g fat (7g sat. fat), 60mg chol., 788mg sod., 29g carb. (3g sugars, 9g fiber), 23g pro. **DIABETIC EXCHANGES** 3 lean meat, 2 starch.

READER REVIEW
"Had a friend's white chili and didn't think I could find another recipe better than hers—boy was I wrong! Both my husband and kids loved this chili. Can't wait to make it for my scrapbooking friends!"
—TRACARL, TASTEOFHOME.COM

❄ VEGAN CABBAGE SOUP

Comforting soups that simmer all day long are staples on cool, busy days. For a heartier version of this vegan cabbage soup, stir in canned beans, such as cannellini or navy.
—Taste of Home *Test Kitchen*

PREP: 15 MIN. • **COOK:** 6 HOURS • **MAKES:** 10 SERVINGS (2½ QT.)

4   **cups vegetable stock**
1   **can (14 oz.) Italian diced tomatoes**
1   **can (6 oz.) tomato paste**
1   **small head cabbage (about 1½ lbs.), shredded**
4   **celery ribs, chopped**
2   **large carrots, chopped**
1   **medium onion, chopped**
2   **garlic cloves, minced**
2   **tsp. Italian seasoning**
½   **tsp. salt**
    Fresh basil, optional

In a 5- or 6-qt. slow cooker, whisk together stock, diced tomatoes and tomato paste. Stir in vegetables, garlic, Italian seasoning and salt. Cook, covered, on low until vegetables are tender, 6-8 hours. If desired, top each serving with fresh basil.

FREEZE OPTION Transfer cooled soup to a freezer container and freeze up to 3 months. To use, thaw in the refrigerator overnight. Reheat on the stovetop or in the microwave; add stock or water as needed.

1 CUP 110 cal., 0 fat (0 sat. fat), 0 chol., 866mg sod., 24g carb. (13g sugars, 6g fiber), 4g pro.

TEST KITCHEN TIPS

• To make a Tex-Mex version of this soup, trade the Italian diced tomatoes and Italian seasoning for Mexican diced tomatoes plus cumin and coriander.

• Make this a heartier soup by adding a can of black beans, kidney beans or lentils.

MAC & CHEESE SOUP

I came across this recipe a few years ago and made some changes to suit my family's tastes. Because it starts with packaged macaroni and cheese, it's ready in a jiffy.
—*Nancy Daugherty, Cortland, OH*

TAKES: 30 MIN. • **MAKES:** 8 SERVINGS (2 QT.)

1 pkg. (14 oz.) deluxe macaroni and cheese dinner mix
9 cups water, divided
1 cup fresh broccoli florets
2 Tbsp. finely chopped onion
1 can (10½ oz.) condensed cheddar cheese soup, undiluted
2½ cups 2% milk
1 cup chopped fully cooked ham

1. Set aside cheese sauce packet from macaroni and cheese mix. In a large saucepan, bring 8 cups water to a boil. Add macaroni; cook for 8-10 minutes or until tender.

2. Meanwhile, in another large saucepan, bring remaining 1 cup water to a boil. Add broccoli and onion; cook, uncovered, for 3 minutes. Stir in the soup, milk, ham and contents of cheese sauce packet; heat through. Drain macaroni; stir into soup.

1 CUP 263 cal., 9g fat (4g sat. fat), 28mg chol., 976mg sod., 32g carb. (6g sugars, 2g fiber), 13g pro.

BROCCOLI MAC & CHEESE SOUP Double the broccoli and omit the ham for a meatless option.

CHICKEN, ASPARAGUS & CORN CHOWDER

Chicken and asparagus make a light, comforting soup that's easy to do with common ingredients. If we have rotisserie chicken, it goes into this soup.
—*Jennifer Vo, Irvine, CA*

TAKES: 30 MIN. • **MAKES:** 4 SERVINGS

- 2 Tbsp. olive oil
- ¾ cup cut fresh asparagus (1-in. pieces)
- 1 small onion, finely chopped
- 2 Tbsp. all-purpose flour
- ½ tsp. salt
- ¼ tsp. garlic powder
- ⅛ to ¼ tsp. pepper
- 1 can (14½ oz.) chicken broth
- ½ cup fat-free half-and-half
- 1½ cups cubed cooked chicken breast
- ¾ cup frozen corn

1. In a large saucepan, heat oil over medium heat. Add the asparagus and onion; cook and stir until tender, 3-4 minutes.
2. Stir in flour, salt, garlic powder and pepper until blended; gradually stir in broth and half-and-half. Bring to a boil, stirring constantly; cook and stir until slightly thickened, 3-5 minutes.
3. Add chicken and corn; heat through.

1 CUP 215 cal., 9g fat (1g sat. fat), 43mg chol., 800mg sod., 15g carb. (4g sugars, 1g fiber), 19g pro.

SPLIT PEA SOUP WITH HAM & JALAPENO

To me, this spicy pea soup is total comfort food. I cook it low and slow all day, and it fills the house with a yummy aroma. It's so good with a nice, crispy baguette.
—Chelsea Tichenor, Huntington Beach, CA

PREP: 15 MIN. • **COOK:** 6 HOURS • **MAKES:** 6 SERVINGS (2¼ QT.)

- 2 smoked ham hocks
- 1 pkg. (16 oz.) dried green split peas
- 4 medium carrots, cut into ½-in. slices
- 1 medium onion, chopped
- 1 jalapeno pepper, seeded and minced
- 3 garlic cloves, minced
- 8 cups water
- 1 tsp. salt
- 1 tsp. pepper

1. In a 4- or 5-qt. slow cooker, combine all ingredients. Cook, covered, on low until meat is tender, 6-8 hours.
2. Remove meat from bones when cool enough to handle; cut ham into small pieces and return to slow cooker.

NOTE Wear disposable gloves when cutting hot peppers; the oils can burn skin. Avoid touching your face.

1½ CUPS 316 cal., 2g fat (0 sat. fat), 9mg chol., 642mg sod., 55g carb. (9g sugars, 21g fiber), 22g pro.

READER REVIEW
"I fixed this and loved it. Left the seeds and ribs in the jalapenos and used two instead of one."
—AN1NETTE, TASTEOFHOME.COM

GARLIC
TORTELLINI
SOUP

GARLIC TORTELLINI SOUP

I like to top bowls of this tasty soup with a little grated Parmesan cheese, and serve it with crusty bread to round out the meal.
—*Donna Morgan, Hendersonville, TN*

TAKES: 25 MIN. • **MAKES:** 6 SERVINGS (1½ QT.)

- 1 Tbsp. butter
- 2 garlic cloves, minced
- 3 cans (14½ oz. each) reduced-sodium chicken broth or vegetable broth
- 1 pkg. (9 oz.) refrigerated cheese tortellini
- 1 can (14½ oz.) diced tomatoes with green chiles, undrained
- 1 pkg. (10 oz.) frozen chopped spinach, thawed and squeezed dry

In a large saucepan, heat butter over medium heat; saute garlic until tender, about 1 minute. Stir in broth; bring to a boil. Add tortellini; cook, uncovered, until tender, 7-9 minutes. Stir in tomatoes and spinach; heat through.

1 CUP 189 cal., 6g fat (3g sat. fat), 23mg chol., 1074mg sod., 25g carb. (2g sugars, 3g fiber), 11g pro.

BEEF NOODLE SOUP

This delicious soup takes only 25 minutes to make—but tastes as if it simmers all day!
—*Margery Bryan, Moses Lake, WA*

TAKES: 25 MIN. • **MAKES:** 8 SERVINGS (2 QT.)

- 1 lb. ground beef
- ½ cup chopped onion
- 2 cans (14½ oz. each) Italian stewed tomatoes
- 2 cans (10½ oz. each) beef broth
- 2 cups frozen mixed vegetables or 1 can (15 oz.) mixed vegetables
- 1 tsp. salt
- ¼ tsp. pepper
- 1 cup uncooked medium egg noodles

In a Dutch oven, cook beef and onion over medium heat until meat is no longer pink, 5-7 minutes, crumbling beef; drain. Add the tomatoes, broth, vegetables and seasonings. Bring to a boil; add noodles. Reduce heat to medium-low; cook, covered, until noodles are tender, 10-15 minutes.

1 CUP 144 cal., 5g fat (2g sat. fat), 32mg chol., 804mg sod., 11g carb. (5g sugars, 2g fiber), 12g pro.

CREAM OF POTATO & CHEDDAR SOUP

The Yukon Gold potatoes my daughter shares from her garden make this soup incredible. Add some cheddar cheese and crisp croutons, and it's just heavenly. Total comfort with the simplicity of good ingredients!

—*Cindi Bauer, Marshfield, WI*

PREP: 25 MIN. • **COOK:** 7½ HOURS • **MAKES:** 11 SERVINGS (2¾ QT.)

8   medium Yukon Gold potatoes, peeled and cubed
1   large red onion, chopped
1   celery rib, chopped
2   cans (14½ oz. each) reduced-sodium chicken broth
1   can (10¾ oz.) condensed cream of celery soup, undiluted
1   tsp. garlic powder
½   tsp. white pepper
1½ cups shredded sharp cheddar cheese
1   cup half-and-half cream
    Optional toppings: Salad croutons, crumbled cooked bacon, chives and additional shredded sharp cheddar cheese

1. Combine the first 7 ingredients in a 4- or 5-qt. slow cooker. Cook, covered, on low until potatoes are tender, 7-9 hours.

2. Stir in cheese and cream. Cover and cook until cheese is melted, 30 minutes longer. Garnish servings with toppings of your choice.

1 CUP 212 cal., 8g fat (5g sat. fat), 28mg chol., 475mg sod., 27g carb. (4g sugars, 3g fiber), 8g pro. **DIABETIC EXCHANGES** 2 starch, 1½ fat.

READER REVIEW

"Bacon adds a wonderful smoky touch. This soup is very creamy and we used skim milk and fat-free half-and-half. We had to substitute cream of chicken soup for the cream of celery, but the switch worked well."

—DANIELLEYLEE, TASTEOFHOME.COM

HEARTY BLACK BEAN SOUP

Cumin and chili powder give spark to this thick, hearty soup. If you have leftover meat—smoked sausage, browned ground beef or roast—toss it in for the last 30 minutes of cooking.
—*Amy Chop, Oak Grove, LA*

PREP: 10 MIN. • **COOK:** 9 HOURS • **MAKES:** 8 SERVINGS

- 3 **medium carrots, halved and thinly sliced**
- 2 **celery ribs, thinly sliced**
- 1 **medium onion, chopped**
- 4 **garlic cloves, minced**
- 1 **can (30 oz.) black beans, rinsed and drained**
- 2 **cans (14½ oz. each) reduced-sodium chicken broth or vegetable broth**
- 1 **can (15 oz.) crushed tomatoes**
- 1½ **tsp. dried basil**
- ½ **tsp. dried oregano**
- ½ **tsp. ground cumin**
- ½ **tsp. chili powder**
- ½ **tsp. hot pepper sauce**
- **Hot cooked rice**

In a 3-qt. slow cooker, combine the first 12 ingredients. Cook, covered, on low until vegetables are tender, 9-11 hours. Serve with rice.

1 CUP 129 cal., 0 fat (0 sat. fat), 0 chol., 627mg sod., 24g carb. (6g sugars, 6g fiber), 8g pro. **DIABETIC EXCHANGES** 1½ starch, 1 lean meat.

READER REVIEW

"I had some bone broth to use so I made a double batch of this soup. Greatly enjoyed the flavors of the spices. Doubled the black beans. Instead of serving with rice, I added the rice (black rice) to the soup. Hearty, for sure, and very delicious. Looking forward to having it again!"
—ANNRMS, TASTEOFHOME.COM

❄ VEGETABLE LENTIL SOUP

Here's a healthy soup that's ideal for vegetarians and those watching their weight. Butternut squash and lentils make it filling, while herbs and other veggies round out the flavor.
—*Mark Morgan, Waterford, WI*

PREP: 15 MIN. • **COOK:** 4½ HOURS • **MAKES:** 6 SERVINGS (ABOUT 2 QT.)

3 cups cubed peeled butternut squash
1 cup chopped carrots
1 cup chopped onion
1 cup dried lentils, rinsed
2 garlic cloves, minced
1 tsp. dried oregano
1 tsp. dried basil
4 cups vegetable broth
1 can (14½ oz.) Italian diced tomatoes, undrained
2 cups frozen cut green beans (about 8 oz.)

1. Place the first 8 ingredients in a 5-qt. slow cooker. Cook, covered, on low until lentils are tender, about 4 hours.

2. Stir in tomatoes and beans. Cook, covered, on high until heated through, about 30 minutes.

FREEZE OPTION Transfer cooled soup to freezer containers and freeze up to 6 months. To use, thaw in the refrigerator overnight. Reheat on the stovetop; add broth or water as needed.

1⅓ CUPS 217 cal., 1g fat (0 sat. fat), 0 chol., 685mg sod., 45g carb. (11g sugars, 8g fiber), 11g pro.

TEST KITCHEN TIP

Give the lentils a quick rinse in a strainer before ading them to the slow cooker to sift out any dust or dirt.

EASY TORTELLINI SPINACH SOUP

This is the easiest soup you will ever make—take it from me! I always keep the ingredients on hand so if I'm feeling under the weather or just plain busy, I can throw together this comforting soup in a flash.

—Angela Lively, Conroe, TX

TAKES: 20 MIN. • **MAKES:** 8 SERVINGS (3 QT.)

16 **frozen fully cooked Italian meatballs (about 1 lb.)**
1 **can (14½ oz.) fire-roasted diced tomatoes, undrained**
¼ **tsp. Italian seasoning**
¼ **tsp. pepper**
2 **cartons (32 oz. each) chicken stock**
2 **cups frozen cheese tortellini (about 8 oz.)**
3 **oz. fresh baby spinach (about 4 cups)**
 Shredded Parmesan cheese, optional

1. Place the first 5 ingredients in a 6-qt. stockpot; bring to a boil. Reduce heat; simmer, covered, 10 minutes.
2. Return to a boil. Add tortellini; cook, uncovered, until meatballs are heated through and tortellini are tender, 3-5 minutes, stirring occasionally.
3. Stir in spinach until wilted. Serve immediately. If desired, top with cheese.

1½ CUPS 177 cal., 8g fat (4g sat. fat), 18mg chol., 949mg sod., 14g carb. (3g sugars, 1g fiber), 12g pro.

TEST KITCHEN TIPS

• Fully cooked Italian sausage, cut into half-moon slices, can be substituted for the meatballs.

• One 9-oz. package refrigerated cheese tortellini may be substituted for 2 cups frozen tortellini.

• Serve the soup soon after adding the tortellini and spinach for the best texture.

ITALIAN CABBAGE SOUP

After doing yard work on a windy day, we love to come in for a light but hearty soup like this one. It's brimming with cabbage, veggies and white beans. Pass the crusty bread!
—*Jennifer Stowell, Deep River, IA*

PREP: 15 MIN. • **COOK:** 6 HOURS • **MAKES:** 8 SERVINGS (2 QT.)

4 **cups chicken stock**
1 **can (6 oz.) tomato paste**
1 **small head cabbage (about 1½ lbs.), shredded**
4 **celery ribs, chopped**
2 **large carrots, chopped**
1 **small onion, chopped**
1 **can (15½ oz.) great northern beans, rinsed and drained**
2 **garlic cloves, minced**
2 **fresh thyme sprigs**
1 **bay leaf**
½ **tsp. salt**
 Shredded Parmesan cheese, optional

1. In a 5- or 6-qt. slow cooker, whisk together stock and tomato paste. Stir in vegetables, beans, garlic and seasonings. Cook, covered, on low until vegetables are tender, 6-8 hours.
2. Remove thyme sprigs and bay leaf. If desired, serve with Parmesan cheese.
1 CUP 111 cal., 0 fat (0 sat. fat), 0 chol., 537mg sod., 21g carb. (7g sugars, 6g fiber), 8g pro. **DIABETIC EXCHANGES** 1½ starch.

ROAST PORK SOUP

This well-seasoned, satisfying soup has a rich, full-bodied broth brimming with tender chunks of pork, potatoes and navy beans. It has been a family favorite for years. Served with cornbread, it's one of our comfort foods in winter.

—*Sue Gulledge, Springville, AL*

PREP: 15 MIN. • **COOK:** 55 MIN. • **MAKES:** 9 SERVINGS (2¼ QT.)

3 cups cubed cooked pork roast
2 medium potatoes, peeled and chopped
1 large onion, chopped
1 can (15 oz.) navy beans, rinsed and drained
1 can (14½ oz.) Italian diced tomatoes, undrained
4 cups water
½ cup unsweetened apple juice
½ tsp. salt
½ tsp. pepper
Minced fresh basil

In a soup kettle or Dutch oven, combine the first 9 ingredients. Bring to a boil. Reduce heat; cover and simmer until vegetables are crisp-tender, about 45 minutes. Sprinkle with basil.

1 CUP 206 cal., 5g fat (2g sat. fat), 42mg chol., 435mg sod., 23g carb. (6g sugars, 4g fiber), 18g pro. **DIABETIC EXCHANGES** 1 starch, 1 vegetable, 1 meat.

READER REVIEW

"Light and yummy. Great way to use up leftover pork roast. I garnished it with fresh parsley because we had no fresh basil. Will make this again."
—ANNRMS, TASTEOFHOME.COM

⑤ ❄ CHORIZO & CHICKPEA SOUP

The chorizo adds its own spice to the broth, creating delicious flavor with no need for more seasonings. And while it's cooking, the whole house smells delicious.

—Jaclyn McKewan, Lancaster, NY

PREP: 15 MIN. • **COOK:** 8¼ HOURS • **MAKES:** 6 SERVINGS

3 cups water
2 celery ribs, chopped
2 fully cooked Spanish chorizo links (3 oz. each), cut into ½-in. pieces
½ cup dried chickpeas or garbanzo beans
1 can (14½ oz.) petite diced tomatoes, undrained
½ cup ditalini or other small pasta
½ tsp. salt

1. Place water, celery, chorizo and chickpeas in a 4- or 5-qt. slow cooker. Cook, covered, on low until chickpeas are tender, 8-10 hours.
2. Stir in tomatoes, pasta and salt; cook, covered, on high until pasta is tender, 15-20 minutes longer.

FREEZE OPTION Freeze cooled soup in freezer containers. To use, partially thaw in refrigerator overnight. Heat through in a saucepan, stirring occasionally; add broth or water if necessary.

1 CUP 180 cal., 8g fat (3g sat. fat), 18mg chol., 569mg sod., 23g carb. (3g sugars, 6g fiber), 9g pro. **DIABETIC EXCHANGES** 1½ starch, 1 high-fat meat.

❄ NAVY BEAN VEGETABLE SOUP

My family really likes bean soup, so I came up with this enticing version. The leftovers are, dare I say, even better the next day!
—*Eleanor Mielke, Mitchell, SD*

PREP: 15 MIN. • **COOK:** 9 HOURS • **MAKES:** 12 SERVINGS (3 QT.)

4 medium carrots, thinly sliced
2 celery ribs, chopped
1 medium onion, chopped
2 cups cubed fully cooked ham
1½ cups dried navy beans
1 envelope vegetable recipe mix (Knorr)
1 envelope onion soup mix
1 bay leaf
½ tsp. pepper
8 cups water

In a 5-qt. slow cooker, combine the first 9 ingredients. Stir in water. Cover and cook on low until beans are tender, 9-10 hours. Discard bay leaf.

FREEZE OPTION Freeze cooled soup in freezer containers. To use, partially thaw in refrigerator overnight. Heat through in a saucepan, stirring occasionally; add water or broth if necessary.

1 CUP 157 cal., 2g fat (1g sat. fat), 12mg chol., 763mg sod., 24g carb. (4g sugars, 8g fiber), 11g pro.

COUNTRY CASSOULET Instead of cubed ham, add 1½ lbs. smoked ham hocks or pork neck bones or a meaty ham bone to slow cooker. Omit onion soup mix; add ¼ tsp. each dried thyme and rosemary. Remove ham bones at end of cooking; stir 2 cups shredded cooked chicken or turkey and ½ lb. sliced smoked sausage into soup. Heat through. Cut meat from ham bones; add to soup.

SLOW-COOKED CORN CHOWDER

I combine and refrigerate the ingredients for this easy chowder the night before. In the morning, I start the slow cooker before I leave for work. When I come home, a hot tasty meal awaits.
—*Mary Hogue, Rochester, PA*

PREP: 10 MIN. • **COOK:** 6 HOURS • **MAKES:** 8 SERVINGS (2 QT.)

2½ cups 2% milk
1 can (14¾ oz.) cream-style corn
1 can (10¾ oz.) condensed cream of mushroom soup, undiluted
1¾ cups frozen corn
1 cup frozen shredded hash brown potatoes
1 cup cubed fully cooked ham
1 large onion, chopped
2 tsp. dried parsley flakes
2 Tbsp. butter
Salt and pepper to taste
Optional toppings:
Crumbled cooked bacon and minced parsley

1. In a 3-qt. slow cooker, combine first 9 ingredients. Cook, covered, on low for 6 hours.
2. Add salt and pepper to taste; if desired, top servings with crumbled bacon and parsley.

1 CUP 196 cal., 8g fat (3g sat. fat), 26mg chol., 687mg sod., 26g carb. (7g sugars, 2g fiber), 9g pro.

DID YOU KNOW?

Dairy-based soups and chowders such as this one do not freeze well. You can store this corn chowder in an airtight container in the refrigerator for 3-4 days.

SLOW-COOKED
PORK STEW, PAGE 147

LAZY-DAY DINNERS

TACO CRESCENT BAKE

A friend shared the recipe with me, and I've prepared it monthly ever since. The crust is made from refrigerated crescent roll dough. While the ground beef is browning, I simply press the dough into a baking dish. Guests always comment on the tasty crust as well as the zesty filling and crunchy topping.

—Patricia Eckard, Singers Glen, VA

PREP: 25 MIN. • **BAKE:** 25 MIN. • **MAKES:** 8 SERVINGS

1 tube (8 oz.) refrigerated crescent rolls
2 cups crushed corn chips, divided
1½ lbs. ground beef
1 can (15 oz.) tomato sauce
1 envelope taco seasoning
1 cup sour cream
1 cup shredded cheddar cheese
Optional: Cubed avocado, chopped tomatoes, and shredded lettuce and cilantro

1. Preheat oven to 350°. Unroll crescent dough into a rectangle; press onto bottom and 1 in. up sides of a greased 13x9-in. baking dish. Seal seams and perforations. Sprinkle with 1 cup chips; set aside.

2. In a large skillet, cook beef over medium heat until no longer pink; drain. Stir in tomato sauce and taco seasoning; bring to a boil. Reduce heat; simmer, uncovered, for 5 minutes. Spoon over chips. Top with sour cream, cheese and remaining chips.

3. Bake, uncovered, 25-30 minutes or until crust is lightly browned. Garnish with optional toppings if desired.

1 PIECE 497 cal., 27g fat (10g sat. fat), 74mg chol., 1183mg sod., 41g carb. (5g sugars, 3g fiber), 24g pro.

EASY DOES IT

Be sure to check out our Lazy-Day Dinners Index, organized by protein source, on pp. 252-253. There, you'll find a convenient breakdown of main dishes featuring beef, pork, poultry, seafood and meatless options.

5i ❄ RANCH PORK ROAST

This simple pork roast with a mild rub is perfect for new cooks. The leftover meat is tender and flavorful enough to be used in countless recipes.

—Taste of Home *Test Kitchen*

PREP: 10 MIN. • **BAKE:** 50 MIN. + STANDING • **MAKES:** 8 SERVINGS

1   boneless pork loin roast
    (2½ lbs.)
2   Tbsp. olive oil
1   Tbsp. ranch salad dressing
    mix
2   tsp. Dijon mustard
1   garlic clove, minced
½   tsp. pepper

1. Preheat oven to 350°. If desired, tie pork with kitchen string at 2-in. intervals to help roast hold its shape. Combine next 5 ingredients; rub over roast. Place on a rack in a shallow roasting pan. Pour 1 cup water into pan.

2. Bake, uncovered, 50-55 minutes or until a thermometer reads 145°. Let stand for 10-15 minutes before slicing.

FREEZE OPTION Freeze cooled sliced pork in freezer containers. To use, partially thaw in refrigerator overnight. Heat through in a covered saucepan, gently stirring; add broth or water if necessary.

4 OZ. COOKED PORK 212 cal., 10g fat (3g sat. fat), 70mg chol., 248mg sod., 2g carb. (0 sugars, 0 fiber), 27g pro. **DIABETIC EXCHANGES** 4 lean meat, ½ fat.

READER REVIEW

"Excellent! The roast was very moist and flavorful, and also quick and easy. We doubled the mixture and made it in the slow cooker with some chicken stock. A definite keeper!"
—CYNANDTOM, TASTEOFHOME.COM

ONE-POT BLACK BEAN ENCHILADA PASTA

I love this cozy dish because it is ready in 30 minutes and is full of healthy ingredients—it has everything a busy weeknight meal calls for.
—*Nora Rushev, Reitnau, Switzerland*

TAKES: 30 MIN. • **MAKES:** 6 SERVINGS

- 4 cups uncooked mini penne or other small pasta
- 4 cups vegetable broth or water
- 1 can (15 oz.) black beans, rinsed and drained
- 1 can (14½ oz.) diced tomatoes, undrained
- 1 medium sweet yellow pepper, chopped
- 1 medium sweet red pepper, chopped
- 1 cup fresh or frozen corn, thawed
- 1 can (10 oz.) enchilada sauce
- 2 Tbsp. taco seasoning
- ½ cup shredded cheddar cheese
  Optional: Fresh cilantro leaves, cherry tomatoes and lime wedges

In a Dutch oven or large skillet, combine first 9 ingredients. Bring to a boil; reduce heat. Simmer, uncovered, until pasta is al dente and sauce has thickened slightly, 12-15 minutes. Add cheese; stir until melted. Serve with optional toppings as desired.

1¾ CUPS 444 cal., 5g fat (2g sat. fat), 9mg chol., 1289mg sod., 84g carb. (8g sugars, 8g fiber), 18g pro.

READER REVIEW
"My family loved this! I followed the directions as given but left out the corn. It was delicious! Using only one pot and having it be done in under 30 minutes was a bonus. I served it with a green salad. I will definitely be making this again."
—SUEFREESE, TASTEOFHOME.COM

CHICKEN
BISCUIT POTPIE

CHICKEN BISCUIT POTPIE

This hearty meal in one takes just 10 minutes to assemble before you can pop it into the oven.
—*Dorothy Smith, El Dorado, AR*

PREP: 10 MIN. • **BAKE:** 25 MIN. • **MAKES:** 4 SERVINGS

1⅔ cups frozen mixed
    vegetables, thawed
1½ cups cubed cooked chicken
1 can (10¾ oz.) condensed
    cream of chicken soup,
    undiluted
¼ tsp. dried thyme
1 cup biscuit/baking mix
½ cup 2% milk
1 large egg

1. Preheat oven to 400°. In a large bowl, combine vegetables, chicken, soup and thyme. Pour into an ungreased deep-dish 9-in. pie plate. Combine biscuit mix, milk and egg; spoon over chicken mixture.

2. Bake until topping is golden brown and a toothpick inserted in center comes out clean, 25-30 minutes.

1 SERVING 376 cal., 14g fat (4g sat. fat), 103mg chol., 966mg sod., 38g carb. (5g sugars, 5g fiber), 23g pro.

🗓 PORK CHOPS & ACORN SQUASH

My husband and I are crazy for the squash we grow in our garden. For a sweet and tangy dish, we slow-cook it with pork chops and orange juice.
—*Mary Johnson, Coloma, WI*

PREP: 15 MIN. • **COOK:** 4 HOURS • **MAKES:** 6 SERVINGS

6 boneless pork loin chops
    (4 oz. each)
2 medium acorn squash,
    halved lengthwise, seeded
    and sliced
½ cup packed brown sugar
2 Tbsp. butter, melted
1 Tbsp. orange juice
¾ tsp. salt
¾ tsp. browning sauce,
    optional
½ tsp. grated orange zest

Place pork chops in a 5-qt. slow cooker; add squash. In a small bowl, mix remaining ingredients; pour over squash. Cook, covered, on low for 4-6 hours or until pork is tender.

1 PORK CHOP WITH ⅔ CUP SQUASH 317 cal., 10g fat (5g sat. fat), 65mg chol., 365mg sod., 34g carb. (22g sugars, 2g fiber), 23g pro.
DIABETIC EXCHANGES 3 lean meat, 2 starch, 1 fat.

⑤i FOIL-BAKED SALMON

Baking salmon in foil is an easy technique that can also be used on the grill. This quick recipe uses lemon zest and slices plus garlic for flavor, but you could also try other citrus fruits, herbs and spices.
—Taste of Home *Test Kitchen*

PREP: 10 MIN. • **BAKE:** 25 MIN. • **MAKES:** 6 SERVINGS

1   salmon fillet (about 2 lbs.)
2   Tbsp. butter, melted
2   garlic cloves, minced
2   tsp. grated lemon zest
1   Tbsp. minced fresh parsley
¾   tsp. salt
¼   tsp. pepper
6   lemon slices

1. Preheat oven to 350°. Line a 15x10x1-in. baking pan with heavy-duty foil; grease lightly. Place salmon skin side down on foil. Combine butter, garlic and lemon zest; drizzle over salmon. Sprinkle with parsley, salt and pepper. Top with lemon. Fold foil around salmon; seal tightly.

2. Bake for 20 minutes. Open foil carefully, allowing steam to escape. Broil 4-6 in. from heat until fish flakes easily with a fork, 3-5 minutes.

4 OZ. COOKED SALMON 273 cal., 18g fat (5g sat. fat), 86mg chol., 402mg sod., 1g carb. (0 sugars, 0 fiber), 26g pro. **DIABETIC EXCHANGES** 4 lean meat, 1 fat.

TUNA MELT SANDWICHES

When our children were young, I often fixed these warm, crunchy sandwiches. They go well with chips and a salad for a quick lunch.
—*Carole Anhalt, Manitowoc, WI*

TAKES: 30 MIN. • **MAKES:** 6 SERVINGS

¾   cup chopped celery
¾   cup diced cheddar cheese
1   can (6 oz.) tuna, drained and flaked
1   small onion, chopped
¼   cup mayonnaise
⅛   tsp. salt
¼   cup butter, softened
6   hamburger buns, split

1. Preheat oven to 350°. In a bowl, combine first 6 ingredients; set aside. Spread butter over cut sides of buns. Spread tuna mixture on bun bottoms; replace tops. Wrap in foil.

2. Bake until cheese is melted, about 15 minutes.

1 SERVING 363 cal., 23g fat (10g sat. fat), 50mg chol., 629mg sod., 23g carb. (4g sugars, 2g fiber), 15g pro.

**FOIL-BAKED
SALMON**

HEARTY BUSY-DAY STEW

When I was still living in Missouri, a friend gave me her family cookbooks. I got the idea for this easy stew from one of those books. The taco seasoning adds just the right touch.
—*Kristen Hills, Layton, UT*

PREP: 10 MIN. • **COOK:** 7½ HOURS • **MAKES:** 6 SERVINGS

1½ lbs. beef stew meat
1½ lbs. potatoes (about 3 medium), peeled and cut into 1-in. cubes
1 can (14½ oz.) diced tomatoes, undrained
1 can (14½ oz.) beef broth
2½ cups fresh baby carrots (about 12 oz.)
1 large tomato, chopped
1 medium onion, chopped
2 Tbsp. taco seasoning
2 garlic cloves, minced
½ tsp. salt
2 Tbsp. cornstarch
2 Tbsp. cold water

1. In a 5- or 6-qt. slow cooker, combine first 10 ingredients. Cook, covered, on low 7-9 hours or until beef and vegetables are tender.

2. In a small bowl, mix cornstarch and water until smooth; gradually stir into stew. Cook, covered, on high 30-45 minutes longer or until stew is slightly thickened.

1¾ CUPS 303 cal., 8g fat (3g sat. fat), 71mg chol., 986mg sod., 32g carb. (8g sugars, 4g fiber), 25g pro

CHEESY TATER TOTS & CANADIAN BACON

This slow-cooker meal was created to pay homage to my favorite style of pizza—Hawaiian with bacon and pineapple. The Tater Tots in this recipe make it family-friendly.
—*Lisa Renshaw, Kansas City, MO*

PREP: 15 MIN. • **COOK:** 4 HOURS + STANDING • **MAKES:** 8 SERVINGS

- 1 pkg. (32 oz.) frozen Tater Tots, thawed
- 8 oz. Canadian bacon, chopped
- 1 cup frozen pepper strips, thawed and chopped
- 1 medium onion, finely chopped
- 1 can (8 oz.) pineapple tidbits, drained
- 2 large eggs
- 3 cans (5 oz. each) evaporated milk
- 1 can (15 oz.) pizza sauce
- 1 cup shredded provolone cheese
- ½ cup grated Parmesan cheese, optional

1. Place half the Tater Tots in a greased 5-qt. slow cooker. Layer with Canadian bacon, pepper, onion and pineapple. Top with remaining Tater Tots. In a large bowl, whisk eggs, milk and pizza sauce; pour over top. Sprinkle with provolone cheese.

2. Cook, covered, on low for 4-5 hours or until heated through. If desired, sprinkle with Parmesan cheese; let stand, covered, 20 minutes.

1½ CUPS 439 cal., 21g fat (8g sat. fat), 85mg chol., 1216mg sod., 43g carb. (14g sugars, 4g fiber), 17g pro.

DID YOU KNOW?

A classic Hawaiian pizza is made with pizza sauce, Canadian bacon or ham, and pineapple. The slightly sweet flavor makes it surprisingly popular in the U.S., especially among kids. According to a GrubHub survey of more than 2.5 million pizza deliveries, orders for Hawaiian pizza trail only behind those for cheese, pepperoni and sausage pies.

MEATY SLOW-COOKED JAMBALAYA

This recipe makes a big batch of delicious, meaty gumbo. Stash some away in the freezer for days you don't feel like cooking.
—*Diane Atherton, Pine Mountain, GA*

PREP: 25 MIN. • **COOK:** 7¼ HOURS • **MAKES:** 12 SERVINGS (3 QT.)

1 can (28 oz.) diced tomatoes, undrained
1 cup reduced-sodium chicken broth
1 large green pepper, chopped
1 medium onion, chopped
2 celery ribs, sliced
½ cup white wine or additional reduced-sodium chicken broth
4 garlic cloves, minced
2 tsp. Cajun seasoning
2 tsp. dried parsley flakes
1 tsp. dried basil
1 tsp. dried oregano
¾ tsp. salt
½ to 1 tsp. cayenne pepper
2 lbs. boneless skinless chicken thighs, cut into 1-in. pieces
1 pkg. (12 oz.) fully cooked andouille or other spicy chicken sausage links
2 lbs. uncooked shrimp (31-40 per lb.), peeled and deveined
8 cups hot cooked brown rice

1. In a large bowl, combine first 13 ingredients. Place chicken and sausage in a 6-qt. slow cooker. Pour tomato mixture over top. Cook, covered, on low until chicken is tender, 7-9 hours.
2. Stir in shrimp. Cook, covered, for 15-20 minutes longer or until shrimp turn pink. Serve with rice.

1 CUP JAMBALAYA WITH ⅔ CUP COOKED RICE 387 cal., 10g fat (3g sat. fat), 164mg chol., 674mg sod., 37g carb. (4g sugars, 4g fiber), 36g pro. **DIABETIC EXCHANGES** 3 lean meat, 2½ starch.

READER REVIEW
"I've made this many times. It's one of our favorite recipes! I prep everything the night before, then throw it into the cooker in the morning. The house smells amazing all day! I use white rice, because that's what we prefer. So much flavor, and it's much easier to use the slow cooker!"
—REBECCA5499, TASTEOFHOME.COM

CORNMEAL-CRUSTED CATFISH

To help breading adhere to the fish, pat the fillets dry and coat lightly with flour before dipping into egg and dredging into the cornmeal coating. Let stand for 5-10 minutes before frying.
—Taste of Home *Test Kitchen*

TAKES: 30 MIN. • **MAKES:** 4 SERVINGS

1 large egg, lightly beaten
2 Tbsp. lemon juice
½ cup all-purpose flour
¼ cup yellow cornmeal
1 tsp. Cajun seasoning
½ tsp. garlic powder
½ tsp. salt
4 catfish fillets (6 oz. each)
3 Tbsp. canola oil

1. In a shallow bowl, combine egg and lemon juice. In another shallow bowl, combine flour, cornmeal, Cajun seasoning, garlic powder and salt. Dip catfish into egg mixture, then coat with cornmeal mixture.

2. In a large skillet, heat oil over medium heat. Fry fillets, 2 at a time, just until fish begins to flake easily with a fork, 5-6 minutes on each side.

1 SERVING 430 cal., 25g fat (5g sat. fat), 133mg chol., 568mg sod., 20g carb. (1g sugars, 1g fiber), 30g pro.

TEST KITCHEN TIP

Paprika or smoked paprika would be a nice addition to this recipe, or you can substitute seafood seasoning for the Cajun seasoning. To give the dish a bright and spicy accent, consider adding a lemon-pepper blend.

POTATO & PEPPER SAUSAGE BAKE

When my family smells this dish baking in the oven, they know they are in for a treat! If you like spice, add a pinch of red pepper flakes or switch the mild Italian sausage to hot Italian sausage.

—*Ashli Claytor, Chesapeake, VA*

PREP: 25 MIN. • **BAKE:** 30 MIN. • **MAKES:** 5 SERVINGS

5 large Yukon Gold potatoes, peeled and cut into 1-in. cubes
1 large sweet orange pepper, sliced
1 large sweet red pepper, sliced
1 shallot, chopped
4 garlic cloves, minced
1 Tbsp. olive oil
2 tsp. paprika
¾ tsp. salt
½ tsp. dried thyme
½ tsp. pepper
1 pkg. (19 oz.) Italian sausage links
   Minced fresh thyme, optional

1. Preheat oven to 400°. Place potatoes, sweet peppers, shallot and garlic in a greased 15x10x1-in. baking pan. Drizzle with oil. Sprinkle with seasonings; toss to coat. Spread evenly over pan, leaving room for sausage. Add sausage to pan.

2. Bake, uncovered, until a thermometer inserted in sausage reads 160° and vegetables are tender, 30-35 minutes. If desired, sprinkle with minced fresh thyme before serving.

1 SAUSAGE LINK WITH ¾ CUP VEGETABLES 446 cal., 26g fat (8g sat. fat), 58mg chol., 1021mg sod., 38g carb. (5g sugars, 4g fiber), 16g pro.

TEST KITCHEN TIP

Arrange the sausages directly onto the pan, instead of on top of the potatoes, to ensure the potatoes cook evenly.

⑤ SLOW-COOKER MEATBALL SANDWICHES

Our approach to meatball sandwiches is a simple one: Cook the meatballs low and slow, load them into hoagie buns, and top them with provolone and pepperoncini.

—*Stacie Nicholls, Spring Creek, NV*

PREP: 5 MIN. • **COOK:** 3 HOURS • **MAKES:** 8 SERVINGS

2 pkg. (12 oz. each) frozen fully cooked Italian meatballs, thawed
2 jars (24 oz. each) marinara sauce
8 hoagie buns, split
8 slices provolone cheese
Sliced pepperoncini, optional

1. Place meatballs and sauce in a 3- or 4-qt. slow cooker. Cook, covered, on low for 3-4 hours or until meatballs are heated through.
2. On each bun bottom, layer cheese, meatballs and, if desired, pepperoncini; replace tops.

1 SANDWICH 526 cal., 20g fat (7g sat. fat), 93mg chol., 1674mg sod., 55g carb. (15g sugars, 4g fiber), 32g pro.

CHICKEN & DUMPLINGS

Perfect for fall nights, my simple version of comforting chicken and dumplings is speedy, low in fat and a delicious one-dish meal.

—*Nancy Tuck, Elk Falls, KS*

TAKES: 30 MIN. • **MAKES:** 6 SERVINGS

3 celery ribs, chopped
2 medium carrots, sliced
3 cans (14½ oz. each) reduced-sodium chicken broth
3 cups cubed cooked chicken breasts
½ tsp. poultry seasoning
⅛ tsp. pepper
1⅔ cups reduced-fat biscuit/baking mix
⅔ cup fat-free milk

1. In a Dutch oven coated with cooking spray, cook and stir celery and carrots over medium heat until tender, about 5 minutes. Stir in broth, chicken and seasonings. Bring to a boil; reduce heat to a gentle simmer.
2. For dumplings, mix biscuit mix and milk until a soft dough forms. Drop by tablespoonfuls on top of simmering liquid. Reduce heat to low; cover and cook for 10-15 minutes or until a toothpick inserted in dumplings comes out clean (do not lift cover during first 10 minutes).

1 CUP 260 cal., 4g fat (1g sat. fat), 54mg chol., 964mg sod., 28g carb. (6g sugars, 2g fiber), 27g pro.

**SLOW-COOKER
MEATBALL SANDWICHES**

SLOW-COOKED PORK STEW

Try this comforting stew that's easy to put together, but it tastes like you've been working hard in the kitchen all day. It's even better served over polenta, egg noodles or mashed potatoes.
—*Nancy Elliott, Houston, TX*

PREP: 15 MIN. • **COOK:** 5 HOURS • **MAKES:** 8 SERVINGS

2 **pork tenderloins (1 lb. each), cut into 2-in. pieces**
1 **tsp. salt**
½ **tsp. pepper**
2 **large carrots, cut into ½-in. slices**
2 **celery ribs, coarsely chopped**
1 **medium onion, coarsely chopped**
3 **cups beef broth**
2 **Tbsp. tomato paste**
⅓ **cup pitted dried plums (prunes), chopped**
4 **garlic cloves, minced**
2 **bay leaves**
1 **fresh rosemary sprig**
1 **fresh thyme sprig**
⅓ **cup Greek olives, optional**
  Chopped fresh parsley, optional
  Hot cooked mashed potatoes, optional

1. Sprinkle pork with salt and pepper; transfer to a 4-qt. slow cooker. Add carrots, celery and onion. In a small bowl, whisk together broth and tomato paste; pour over vegetables. Add plums, garlic, bay leaves, rosemary, thyme and, if desired, olives. Cook, covered, on low for 5-6 hours or until meat and vegetables are tender.

2. Discard bay leaves, rosemary and thyme. If desired, sprinkle stew with parsley and serve with potatoes.

1 CUP 177 cal., 4g fat (1g sat. fat), 64mg chol., 698mg sod., 9g carb. (4g sugars, 1g fiber), 24g pro. **DIABETIC EXCHANGES** 3 lean meat, ½ starch.

READER REVIEW
"This was a creative, delicious recipe. It was my first time making a pork stew, and I absolutely loved this original idea. Very good flavors and seasonings in this recipe."
—SREMENEK, TASTEOFHOME.COM

㊶ ❄ BEEF BRISKET TACOS

Birthday parties back home were big gatherings of cousins, aunts, uncles, grandparents and anyone else we considered family. As soon as guests arrived, hot pans of shredded brisket, or *carne deshebrada,* appeared, along with huge bowls of salads, frijoles, tostadas and salsas. Brisket was the dish we always counted on because it could be made in the oven or a slow cooker.
—Yvette Marquez, Littleton, CO

PREP: 15 MIN. + MARINATING • **COOK:** 8 HOURS • **MAKES:** 10 SERVINGS

1 bottle (12 oz.) beer or nonalcoholic beer
1 cup brisket marinade sauce or liquid smoke plus 1 Tbsp. salt
2 bay leaves
½ tsp. salt
½ tsp. pepper
1 fresh beef brisket (3-4 lbs.), fat trimmed
20 corn tortillas (6 in.), warmed
Optional: Shredded cheddar cheese, lime wedges, media crema table cream, fresh cilantro leaves, thinly sliced green onions, jalapeno slices and salsa

1. In a bowl or shallow dish, combine first 5 ingredients. Add brisket; turn to coat. Cover and refrigerate overnight.

2. Transfer brisket and marinade to a 6-qt. slow cooker. Cook, covered, on low until tender, 8-10 hours. Remove meat; discard bay leaves. Reserve juices in slow cooker. When cool enough to handle, shred meat with 2 forks. Return to slow cooker.

3. Using tongs, serve shredded brisket in tortillas. Add toppings as desired.

FREEZE OPTION Once cooled, freeze meat mixture and juices in airtight freezer containers. To use, partially thaw meat and juices in refrigerator overnight, then heat through in a saucepan, stirring occasionally.

2 TACOS 278 cal., 7g fat (2g sat. fat), 58mg chol., 947mg sod., 21g carb. (0 sugars, 3g fiber), 31g pro.

EASY DOES IT

There are endless topping options for brisket tacos! In addition to cheese, cilantro and sour cream, spoon on some pico de gallo, mild tomato salsa or guacamole. Consider adding thinly sliced radishes or green onions for a bit of heat and crunch.

GREEN CHILE CHOPS WITH SWEET POTATOES

It takes only a few minutes to combine the ingredients in a slow cooker, and you'll have a satisfying, healthy dinner waiting for you at the end of the day. We like to serve ours with fresh-baked garlic bread.

—Marina Ashworth, Denver, CO

PREP: 20 MIN. • **COOK:** 6 HOURS • **MAKES:** 4 SERVINGS

3 medium sweet potatoes, peeled and cut into ½-in. slices
1 large onion, chopped
1 large green pepper, coarsely chopped
1½ cups frozen corn
½ tsp. salt
¼ tsp. pepper
4 boneless pork loin chops (6 oz. each)
1 can (10 oz.) mild green enchilada sauce
½ cup sour cream
2 Tbsp. reduced-sodium teriyaki sauce

1. In a 6-qt. slow cooker, combine sweet potatoes, onion, green pepper, corn, salt and pepper. Top with pork chops. In a small bowl, mix enchilada sauce, sour cream and teriyaki sauce; pour over meat.

2. Cook, covered, on low until meat is tender, 6-8 hours.

1 SERVING 495 cal., 17g fat (7g sat. fat), 102mg chol., 909mg sod., 45g carb. (16g sugars, 5g fiber), 39g pro.

MOIST ITALIAN TURKEY BREAST

This recipe makes some of the juiciest turkey I've ever eaten. High in lean protein, it's a smart entree for a special occasion.

—Jessica Kunz, Springfield, IL

PREP: 25 MIN. • **COOK:** 5 HOURS + STANDING • **MAKES:** 12 SERVINGS

1 lb. carrots, cut into 2-in. pieces
2 medium onions, cut into wedges
3 celery ribs, cut into 2-in. pieces
1 can (14½ oz.) chicken broth
1 bone-in turkey breast (6-7 lbs.), thawed and skin removed
2 Tbsp. olive oil
1½ tsp. seasoned salt
1 tsp. Italian seasoning
½ tsp. pepper

1. Place vegetables and broth in a 6- or 7-qt. slow cooker; top with turkey breast. Brush turkey with oil; sprinkle with seasonings.

2. Cook, covered, on low for 5-6 hours or until a thermometer inserted in turkey reads at least 170°. Remove turkey from slow cooker; let stand, covered, 15 minutes before carving. Serve with vegetables. If desired, strain cooking juices and thicken for gravy.

1 SERVING 360 cal., 15g fat (4g sat. fat), 123mg chol., 477mg sod., 6g carb. (3g sugars, 2g fiber), 48g pro.

SUMMER STRAWBERRY SALAD WITH CHICKEN

I love the Strawberry Poppyseed Salad at Panera Bread but can't always make it to the restaurant, so I created my own version. It's quick, delicious and ready when I want it.
—*Diane Marie Sahley, Lakewood, OH*

TAKES: 15 MIN. • **MAKES:** 4 SERVINGS

1 pkg. (10 oz.) romaine salad mix (about 8 cups)
1 lb. sliced cooked chicken
1½ cups sliced fresh strawberries
1 cup pineapple tidbits, drained
½ cup mandarin oranges, drained
½ cup fresh blueberries
½ cup chopped pecans
½ cup poppyseed salad dressing

Arrange romaine on 4 serving plates. Top with chicken, strawberries, pineapple, mandarin oranges and blueberries. Sprinkle with pecans. Drizzle with dressing.

2 CUPS 557 cal., 31g fat (5g sat. fat), 111mg chol., 329mg sod., 34g carb. (25g sugars, 5g fiber), 37g pro.

BAKED FISH & RICE

The first time I tried this meal-in-one dish, it was an instant hit at our house. Fish and rice are a tasty change of pace from traditional meat-and-potato fare.
—*Jo Groth, Plainfield, IA*

PREP: 10 MIN. • **BAKE:** 35 MIN. • **MAKES:** 4 SERVINGS

1½ cups chicken broth
½ cup uncooked long grain rice
¼ tsp. Italian seasoning
¼ tsp. garlic powder
3 cups frozen chopped broccoli, thawed and drained
1 Tbsp. grated Parmesan cheese
1 can (2.8 oz.) french-fried onions, divided
1 lb. cod fillets
Dash paprika
½ cup shredded cheddar cheese

1. In a large saucepan, combine chicken broth, rice, Italian seasoning and garlic powder; bring to a boil. Transfer to a greased 11x7-in. baking dish. Cover and bake at 375° for 10 minutes. Add broccoli, Parmesan cheese and half the onions. Top with fish fillets; sprinkle with paprika.
2. Cover and bake 20-25 minutes longer or until fish flakes easily with a fork. Uncover; sprinkle with cheddar cheese and remaining onions. Return to the oven for 3 minutes or until cheese is melted.

1 SERVING 392 cal., 16g fat (6g sat. fat), 81mg chol., 722mg sod., 31g carb. (2g sugars, 2g fiber), 29g pro.

TEST KITCHEN TIP

Fish stays the freshest when stored on ice. To keep it ice-cold without mess or damaging the fish's texture, place frozen gel packs or blue ice blocks in a container, then top with the wrapped fish. Place it in the meat drawer. Use within a few days. Wash the ice packs with hot soapy water before reuse.

ZA'ATAR CHICKEN

It's hard to find a dinner that both my husband and kids will enjoy—and even harder to find one that's fast and easy. This is it! No matter how much I make of this dish, it's gone to the last bite.
—*Esther Erani, Brooklyn, NY*

PREP: 20 MIN. • **COOK:** 5 HOURS • **MAKES:** 6 SERVINGS

¼ cup za'atar seasoning
¼ cup olive oil
3 tsp. dried oregano
1 tsp. salt
½ tsp. ground cumin
½ tsp. ground turmeric
3 lbs. bone-in chicken thighs
1 cup pimiento-stuffed
   olives
½ cup dried apricots
½ cup pitted dried plums
   (prunes)
¼ cup water
   Hot cooked basmati rice,
   optional

1. In a large bowl, combine first 6 ingredients. Add chicken; toss to coat.

2. Arrange olives, apricots and plums in bottom of a 4- or 5-qt. slow cooker. Add ¼ cup water; top with chicken. Cook, covered, on low until chicken is tender, 5-6 hours. If desired, serve with rice.

1 SERVING 484 cal., 32g fat (7g sat. fat), 107mg chol., 1367mg sod., 18g carb. (10g sugars, 2g fiber), 30g pro.

TEST KITCHEN TIPS

• To make your own za'atar seasoning, mix 1 Tbsp. each of sesame seeds, chopped fresh oregano, ground sumac and ground cumin with 1 tsp. each of kosher salt and fresh-ground pepper.

• Za'atar seasoning may become your new favorite spice. Add it to melted butter and serve over popcorn, mix it with olive oil for a dipping sauce, or toss it with potatoes prior to roasting.

⑤ BURRATA PASTA

This garlicky, cheesy pasta dish is a quick path to a weeknight dinner. Burrata is a semisoft creamy cheese with a subtle sweetness.
—Taste of Home *Test Kitchen*

TAKES: 20 MIN. • **MAKES:** 4 SERVINGS

- 8 oz. uncooked fusilli pasta
- 3 Tbsp. olive oil
- 2 cups cherry tomatoes, halved
- 4 garlic cloves, minced
- ½ tsp. salt
- ¼ tsp. pepper
- 8 oz. burrata cheese, torn
- ¼ cup minced fresh basil
  Crushed red pepper flakes, optional

1. Cook pasta according to package directions.
2. Meanwhile, in a large skillet, heat oil over medium heat. Add tomatoes; cook and stir until just softened, 3-4 minutes. Add garlic, salt and pepper; cook 1 minute longer.
3. Drain pasta, reserving ¼ cup cooking liquid. Add pasta and cooking liquid to tomato mixture; stir to combine. Remove from heat. Stir in burrata and basil; garnish with red pepper flakes if desired.

1 CUP 498 cal., 27g fat (10g sat. fat), 40mg chol., 390mg sod., 47g carb. (6g sugars, 3g fiber), 18g pro.

⑤ ❄ EASY SALSA SLOPPY JOES

I created these sandwiches when I realized I did not have a can of sloppy joe sauce. The sweet brown sugar in this recipe complements the tangy salsa.
—*Krista Collins, Concord, NC*

TAKES: 20 MIN. • **MAKES:** 8 SERVINGS

- 1 lb. ground beef
- 1⅓ cups salsa
- 1 can (10¾ oz.) condensed tomato soup, undiluted
- 1 Tbsp. brown sugar
- 8 hamburger buns, split

In a large skillet, cook beef over medium heat until no longer pink, breaking into crumbles; drain. Stir in salsa, soup and brown sugar. Cover and simmer 10 minutes or until heated through. Serve on buns.

FREEZE OPTION Cool and place in a freezer container; freeze up to 3 months. To use, thaw beef mixture in refrigerator; place in a saucepan and heat through. Serve on buns.

1 SANDWICH 271 cal., 8g fat (3g sat. fat), 35mg chol., 620mg sod., 32g carb. (9g sugars, 1g fiber), 15g pro.

BURRATA PASTA

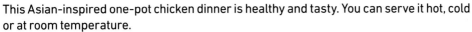

GINGER CHICKEN & QUINOA STEW

This Asian-inspired one-pot chicken dinner is healthy and tasty. You can serve it hot, cold or at room temperature.

—Doris Kwon, Newport Coast, CA

PREP: 25 MIN. • **COOK:** 3½ HOURS • **MAKES:** 8 SERVINGS

2 lbs. boneless skinless chicken thighs, cut into 1-in. pieces
1 cup quinoa, rinsed
1 medium onion, cut into 1-in. pieces
1 medium sweet yellow pepper, cut into 1-in. pieces
1 medium sweet red pepper, cut into 1-in. pieces
2 cups chicken broth
½ cup honey
⅓ cup reduced-sodium soy sauce
¼ cup mirin (sweet rice wine) or sherry
1 Tbsp. minced fresh gingerroot
2 garlic cloves, minced
¼ to 1 tsp. crushed red pepper flakes
1 can (8 oz.) unsweetened pineapple chunks, drained
3 green onions, thinly sliced
2 tsp. sesame seeds

1. Place chicken in a 4- or 5-qt. slow cooker. Top with quinoa, onion and peppers. In a medium bowl, whisk chicken broth, honey, soy sauce, mirin, ginger, garlic and red pepper flakes; pour into slow cooker.

2. Cook, covered, on low for 3½-4 hours or until chicken is tender. Serve with pineapple, green onions and sesame seeds.

1 CUP 373 cal., 10g fat (3g sat. fat), 77mg chol., 696mg sod., 43g carb. (26g sugars, 3g fiber), 26g pro.

SPICY TUNA CRUNCH WRAPS

These quick-to-fix wraps are ideal for lunch or dinner. They're versatile too—you can replace the tuna with chicken, turkey or ham. Adapt them to whatever you have on hand for a fun alternative to sandwiches.

—*Amy Smeltzer, Frostburg, MD*

TAKES: 15 MIN. • **MAKES:** 4 SERVINGS

4 **pouches (2.6 oz. each) sweet and spicy chunk light tuna**
1½ **cups coleslaw mix**
⅓ **cup chopped salted peanuts**
1 **Tbsp. rice vinegar**
¼ **tsp. crushed red pepper flakes**
⅛ **tsp. pepper**
12 **Bibb or Boston lettuce leaves (about 1 medium) Reduced-sodium soy sauce**

In a small bowl, combine first 6 ingredients; toss lightly to combine. Serve in lettuce leaves with soy sauce.

3 LETTUCE WRAPS 179 cal., 7g fat (1g sat. fat), 35mg chol., 495mg sod., 10g carb. (6g sugars, 2g fiber), 20g pro. **DIABETIC EXCHANGES** 3 lean meat, 1 fat, ½ starch.

SWEET & SOUR BRISKET

Here's one dish that never gets old in our house. It's tender and juicy, with a sweet and sour twist. We'd eat it every night if we could!

—*Jolie Albertazzie, Moreno Valley, CA*

PREP: 15 MIN. • **COOK:** 8 HOURS • **MAKES:** 10 SERVINGS

1   **can (28 oz.) crushed tomatoes**
1   **medium onion, halved and thinly sliced**
½   **cup raisins**
¼   **cup packed brown sugar**
2   **Tbsp. lemon juice**
3   **garlic cloves, minced**
1   **fresh beef brisket (3 lbs.)**
½   **tsp. salt**
¼   **tsp. pepper**

1. In a small bowl, combine tomatoes, onion, raisins, brown sugar, lemon juice and garlic. Pour half into a 4- or 5-qt. slow cooker coated with cooking spray.

2. Sprinkle meat with salt and pepper. Transfer to slow cooker. Top with remaining tomato mixture. Cook, covered, on low until meat is tender, 8-10 hours.

3. Remove brisket to a serving platter and keep warm. Skim fat from cooking juices. Thinly slice meat across the grain. Serve with tomato mixture.

NOTE This is a fresh beef brisket, not corned beef.

4 OZ. COOKED BEEF WITH ⅓ CUP SAUCE 248 cal., 6g fat (2g sat. fat), 58mg chol., 272mg sod., 19g carb. (11g sugars, 2g fiber), 30g pro. **DIABETIC EXCHANGES** 4 lean meat, 1 starch.

CHEESE-STUFFED BURGERS FOR TWO

Here's a sandwich that does traditional burgers one better—with a surprise pocket of cheddar! My family really enjoys the melted cheese center.
—*Janet Wood, Windham, NH*

TAKES: 25 MIN. • **MAKES:** 2 SERVINGS

- 1 **Tbsp. finely chopped onion**
- 1 **Tbsp. ketchup**
- 1 **tsp. prepared mustard**
- ¼ **tsp. salt**
- ⅛ **tsp. pepper**
- ½ **lb. lean ground beef (90% lean)**
- ¼ **cup finely shredded cheddar cheese**
- 2 **hamburger buns, split**
  Optional: Lettuce leaves and tomato slices

1. In a small bowl, combine first 5 ingredients. Crumble beef over mixture and mix lightly but thoroughly. Shape into 4 thin patties. Sprinkle cheese over 2 patties; top with remaining patties and press edges firmly to seal.

2. Grill burgers, covered, over medium heat 5-6 minutes on each side or until a thermometer reads 160°. Serve on buns, with lettuce and tomato if desired.

1 BURGER 357 cal., 15g fat (7g sat. fat), 84mg chol., 787mg sod., 25g carb. (4g sugars, 1g fiber), 28g pro. **DIABETIC EXCHANGES** 3 lean meat, 1½ starch, 1½ fat.

READER REVIEW

"Mmmm! Mmmm! These are so good! We stuffed them with blue cheese crumbles, and they were tasty! Five stars from me!"
—STEPHANIE_SIMS20, TASTEOFHOME.COM

CAROLINA SHRIMP & CHEDDAR GRITS

Shrimp and grits are a house favorite—if only we could agree on a recipe. I stirred things up with cheddar cheese and Cajun seasoning to find a winner.
—*Charlotte Price, Raleigh, NC*

PREP: 15 MIN. • **COOK:** 2¾ HOURS • **MAKES:** 6 SERVINGS

1 cup uncooked stone-ground grits
1 large garlic clove, minced
½ tsp. salt
¼ tsp. pepper
4 cups water
2 cups shredded cheddar cheese
¼ cup butter, cubed
1 lb. peeled and deveined cooked shrimp (31-40 per lb.)
2 medium tomatoes, seeded and finely chopped
4 green onions, finely chopped
2 Tbsp. chopped fresh parsley
4 tsp. lemon juice
2 to 3 tsp. Cajun seasoning

1. Place first 5 ingredients in a 3-qt. slow cooker; stir to combine. Cook, covered, on high until water is absorbed and grits are tender, 2½-3 hours, stirring every 45 minutes.
2. Stir in cheese and butter until melted. Stir in remaining ingredients; cook, covered, on high until heated through, 15-30 minutes.

1⅓ CUPS 417 cal., 22g fat (13g sat. fat), 175mg chol., 788mg sod., 27g carb. (2g sugars, 2g fiber), 27g pro.

EASY DOES IT

To quickly seed a tomato, cut it into wedges. Swipe your finger over each wedge to remove the gel pocket and seeds. This is nice for when you don't need perfectly seeded tomatoes.

❄ FORGOTTEN JAMBALAYA

During chilly times of the year, I fix this jambalaya at least once a month. It's so easy—just chop the vegetables, dump everything in the slow cooker and forget it! Even my sons, who are picky about spicy things, like this dish.
—*Cindi Coss, Coppell, TX*

PREP: 35 MIN. • **COOK:** 4¼ HOURS • **MAKES:** 11 SERVINGS

1 can (14½ oz.) diced tomatoes, undrained
1 can (14½ oz.) beef or chicken broth
1 can (6 oz.) tomato paste
3 celery ribs, chopped
2 medium green peppers, chopped
1 medium onion, chopped
5 garlic cloves, minced
3 tsp. dried parsley flakes
2 tsp. dried basil
1½ tsp. dried oregano
1¼ tsp. salt
½ tsp. cayenne pepper
½ tsp. hot pepper sauce
1 lb. boneless skinless chicken breasts, cut into 1-in. cubes
1 lb. smoked sausage, halved and cut into ¼-in. slices
½ lb. uncooked shrimp (31-40 per lb.), peeled and deveined
Hot cooked rice

1. In a 5-qt. slow cooker, combine tomatoes, broth and tomato paste. Stir in celery, green peppers, onion, garlic, seasonings and pepper sauce. Stir in chicken and sausage.

2. Cover and cook on low for 4-6 hours or until chicken is no longer pink. Stir in shrimp. Cover and cook for 15-30 minutes longer or until shrimp turn pink. Serve with rice.

FREEZE OPTION Place individual portions of cooled stew in freezer containers and freeze. To use, partially thaw in refrigerator overnight. Heat through in a saucepan, stirring occasionally and adding water if necessary.

1 CUP 230 cal., 13g fat (5g sat. fat), 75mg chol., 1016mg sod., 9g carb. (5g sugars, 2g fiber), 20g pro.

DID YOU KNOW?

Oregano comes in two types. The sweet Mediterranean one is often simply labeled oregano. It belongs to the mint family. Mexican oregano, a member of the verbena family, has a more intense flavor and citrusy notes.

ONE-PAN ROTINI WITH TOMATO CREAM SAUCE

I like to make one-pan recipes and this one was proclaimed a winner by my family. Bonus: It's also easy to clean up. Serve with crusty bread to dip into the sauce.
—*Angela Lively, Conroe, TX*

PREP: 15 MIN. • **COOK:** 30 MIN. • **MAKES:** 6 SERVINGS

1   lb. lean ground beef (90% lean)
1   medium onion, chopped
2   garlic cloves, minced
1   tsp. Italian seasoning
½   tsp. pepper
¼   tsp. salt
2   cups beef stock
1   can (14½ oz.) fire-roasted diced tomatoes, undrained
2   cups uncooked spiral pasta
1   cup frozen peas
1   cup heavy whipping cream
½   cup grated Parmesan cheese

1. In a large skillet, cook beef and onion over medium heat until beef is no longer pink and onion is tender, 5-10 minutes, breaking beef into crumbles; drain. Add garlic and seasonings; cook 1 minute longer. Add stock and tomatoes; bring to a boil. Add pasta and peas; reduce heat. Simmer, covered, until pasta is tender, 10-12 minutes.

2. Gradually stir in cream and cheese; heat through (do not allow to boil).

1 CUP 443 cal., 23g fat (13g sat. fat), 98mg chol., 646mg sod., 33g carb. (6g sugars, 3g fiber), 25g pro.

TEST KITCHEN TIPS

• Even if all the noodles aren't totally submerged in liquid when added to the pan, they will still cook through.

• For an extra boost of flavor, stir in cooked sausage and serve with additional cheese.

GARDEN CHICKEN CACCIATORE

Treat company to this perfect Italian meal. You will have time to visit with your guests while it simmers, and it often earns rave reviews. I serve it with couscous, green beans and a dry red wine. *Mangia!*

—Martha Schirmacher, Sterling Heights, MI

PREP: 15 MIN. • **COOK:** 8½ HOURS • **MAKES:** 12 SERVINGS

12 boneless skinless chicken thighs (about 3 lbs.)
2 medium green peppers, chopped
1 can (14½ oz.) diced tomatoes with basil, oregano and garlic, undrained
1 can (6 oz.) tomato paste
1 medium onion, chopped
½ cup reduced-sodium chicken broth
¼ cup dry red wine or additional reduced-sodium chicken broth
3 garlic cloves, minced
¾ tsp. salt
⅛ tsp. pepper
2 Tbsp. cornstarch
2 Tbsp. cold water
   Minced fresh parsley, optional

1. Place chicken in a 4- or 5-qt. slow cooker. In a medium bowl, combine green peppers, tomatoes, tomato paste, onion, broth, wine, garlic, salt and pepper; pour over chicken. Cook, covered, on low for 8-10 hours or until chicken is tender.

2. In a small bowl, mix cornstarch and water until smooth; gradually stir into slow cooker. Cook, covered, on high for 30 minutes longer or until sauce is thickened. If desired, sprinkle with parsley before serving.

3 OZ. COOKED CHICKEN WITH ABOUT ½ CUP SAUCE 207 cal., 9g fat (2g sat. fat), 76mg chol., 410mg sod., 8g carb. (4g sugars, 1g fiber), 23g pro. **DIABETIC EXCHANGES** 3 lean meat, 1 vegetable, ½ fat.

SLOW-COOKED PORK TACOS

Sometimes I'll substitute Bibb lettuce leaves for the tortillas to make crunchy lettuce wraps instead of tacos.

—Kathleen Wolf, Naperville, IL

PREP: 20 MIN. • **COOK:** 4 HOURS • **MAKES:** 10 SERVINGS

2 lbs. boneless pork sirloin chops, cut into 2-in. pieces
1½ cups salsa verde
1 medium sweet red pepper, chopped
1 medium onion, chopped
¼ cup chopped dried apricots
2 Tbsp. lime juice
2 garlic cloves, minced
1 tsp. ground cumin
½ tsp. salt
¼ tsp. white pepper
Dash hot pepper sauce
10 flour tortillas (8 in.), warmed
Optional toppings: Chopped tomatoes, cubed avocado, reduced-fat sour cream, shredded reduced-fat cheddar cheese and sliced green onions

1. In a 3-qt. slow cooker, combine all ingredients except tortillas and toppings. Cook, covered, on high until meat is tender, 4-5 hours.
2. Shred pork with 2 forks. Serve in tortillas; top as desired.

1 TACO 310 cal., 9g fat (3g sat. fat), 55mg chol., 596mg sod., 34g carb. (4g sugars, 2g fiber), 23g pro. **DIABETIC EXCHANGES** 3 lean meat, 2 starch.

READER REVIEW
"This was amazing! The best thing I have ever made! Five stars is not enough for this. My husband and kids loved it, saying it's their favorite dinner! I'll make it again."
—TERESA_ELWEL, TASTEOFHOME.COM

❄ PRESSURE-COOKER SPICE-BRAISED POT ROAST

Herbs and spices give the beef an excellent flavor. I often serve this roast over noodles or with mashed potatoes, using the juices as a gravy.
—*Loren Martin, Big Cabin, OK*

PREP: 15 MIN. • **COOK:** 50 MIN. + RELEASING • **MAKES:** 8 SERVINGS

1 **boneless beef chuck roast (2½ lbs.), halved**
1 **can (14½ oz.) diced tomatoes, undrained**
1 **medium onion, chopped**
½ **cup water**
¼ **cup white vinegar**
3 **Tbsp. tomato puree**
1 **Tbsp. poppy seeds**
1 **bay leaf**
2¼ **tsp. sugar**
2 **tsp. Dijon mustard**
2 **garlic cloves, minced**
½ **tsp. salt**
½ **tsp. ground ginger**
½ **tsp. dried rosemary, crushed**
½ **tsp. lemon juice**
¼ **tsp. ground cumin**
¼ **tsp. ground turmeric**
¼ **tsp. crushed red pepper flakes**
⅛ **tsp. ground cloves**
  Hot cooked egg noodles

1. Place roast in a 6-qt. electric pressure cooker. Mix all remaining ingredients except noodles; pour over roast. Lock lid; close pressure-release valve. Adjust to pressure-cook on high for 50 minutes. Let pressure release naturally. A thermometer inserted in beef should read at least 145°.

2. Discard bay leaf. If desired, skim fat and thicken cooking juices. Serve pot roast with noodles and juices.

FREEZE OPTION Place pot roast in freezer containers; top with cooking juices. Cool and freeze. To use, partially thaw in refrigerator overnight. Heat through in a covered saucepan, stirring gently; add water if necessary.

1 SERVING 272 cal., 14g fat (5g sat. fat), 92mg chol., 320mg sod., 6g carb. (4g sugars, 1g fiber), 29g pro. **DIABETIC EXCHANGES** 4 lean meat, ½ starch.

MEDITERRANEAN SHRIMP & PASTA

Sun-dried tomatoes and curry take center stage in this dish that's loaded with tender shrimp and pasta.

—*Shirley Kunde, Rhinelander, WI*

PREP: 15 MIN. • **COOK:** 20 MIN. • **MAKES:** 4 SERVINGS

1 cup boiling water
½ cup dry-pack sun-dried tomatoes, chopped
6 oz. uncooked fettuccine
1 can (8 oz.) tomato sauce
2 Tbsp. clam juice
2 Tbsp. unsweetened apple juice
1 tsp. curry powder
¼ tsp. pepper
1 lb. fresh asparagus, trimmed and cut into 1-in. pieces
1 Tbsp. olive oil
½ cup thinly sliced green onions
2 garlic cloves, minced
1 lb. uncooked shrimp (31-40 per lb.), peeled and deveined

1. In a small bowl, pour boiling water over sun-dried tomatoes; let stand for 2 minutes. Drain and set aside. Cook fettuccine according to package directions.

2. Meanwhile, in a small bowl, combine tomato sauce, clam juice, apple juice, curry powder and pepper; set aside. In a large nonstick skillet coated with cooking spray, cook asparagus in oil for 2 minutes. Add green onions and garlic; cook and stir for 1 minute longer.

3. Stir in shrimp. Cook and stir 3 minutes longer or until shrimp turn pink. Stir in tomato sauce mixture and sun-dried tomatoes; heat through. Drain fettuccine and add to skillet; toss to coat.
1½ CUPS 368 cal., 6g fat (1g sat. fat), 173mg chol., 702mg sod., 46g carb. (8g sugars, 5g fiber), 32g pro. **DIABETIC EXCHANGES** 3 starch, 3 lean meat, ½ fat.

READER REVIEW
"Great recipe. Subtle curry flavor combines well with the asparagus, shrimp and sun-dried tomatoes. This is a hit with the whole family."
—JRAYSHERRY, TASTEOFHOME.COM

❄ POTLUCK TACO CASSEROLE

This is the dish I most often take to potlucks, and the pan comes home empty every time.
—*Kim Stoller, Smithville, OH*

PREP: 25 MIN. • **BAKE:** 20 MIN. • **MAKES:** 8 SERVINGS

2 lbs. ground beef
2 envelopes taco seasoning
4 large eggs
¾ cup 2% milk
1¼ cups biscuit/baking mix
Dash pepper
½ cup sour cream
2 to 3 cups chopped lettuce
¾ cup chopped tomato
¼ cup chopped green pepper
2 green onions, chopped
2 cups shredded cheddar cheese

1. Preheat oven to 400°. In a large skillet, cook beef over medium heat until no longer pink, 10-12 minutes, breaking into crumbles; drain. Add taco seasoning and prepare according to package directions. Spoon meat into a greased 13x9-in. baking dish.

2. In a large bowl, beat eggs and milk. Stir in biscuit mix and pepper. Pour over meat. Bake, uncovered, 20-25 minutes or until golden brown. Cool 5-10 minutes.

3. Spread sour cream over top; sprinkle with lettuce, tomato, green pepper, onions and cheese.

FREEZE OPTION Cool baked casserole; cover and freeze. To use, partially thaw in refrigerator overnight. Remove from refrigerator 30 minutes before baking. Preheat oven to 350°. Unwrap casserole; reheat on a lower oven rack until heated through and a thermometer inserted in center reads 165°. Cool for 5-10 minutes, then top as directed.

1 SERVING 472 cal., 27g fat (14g sat. fat), 205mg chol., 1360mg sod., 24g carb. (3g sugars, 1g fiber), 32g pro.

EASY DOES IT

For individual portions that kids will love, bake the casserole in greased muffin cups until golden brown, 15-20 minutes.

STEPHANIE'S SLOW-COOKER STEW

Start this warming one-pot meal before you head out for the day. By the time you get home, the well-seasoned meat will be tender and mouthwatering.

—*Stephanie Rabbitt-Schapp, Cincinnati, OH*

PREP: 20 MIN. • **COOK:** 7½ HOURS • **MAKES:** 5 SERVINGS

1 lb. beef stew meat
2 medium potatoes, peeled and cubed
1 can (14½ oz.) beef broth
1 can (11½ oz.) V8 juice
2 celery ribs, chopped
2 medium carrots, chopped
1 medium sweet onion, chopped
3 bay leaves
½ tsp. salt
½ tsp. dried thyme
½ tsp. chili powder
¼ tsp. pepper
2 Tbsp. cornstarch
1 Tbsp. cold water
½ cup frozen corn
½ cup frozen peas

1. In a 3-qt. slow cooker, combine first 12 ingredients. Cover and cook on low for 7-8 hours or until meat is tender. Discard bay leaves.

2. In a small bowl, combine cornstarch and water until smooth; stir into stew. Add corn and peas. Cover and cook on high for 30 minutes or until thickened.

1⅓ CUPS 273 cal., 7g fat (2g sat. fat), 56mg chol., 865mg sod., 31g carb. (9g sugars, 4g fiber), 22g pro. **DIABETIC EXCHANGES** 3 lean meat, 2 vegetable, 1 starch.

READER REVIEW
"I made this last night for us and we enjoyed it. I think the V8 juice added an extra depth of flavor to this stew. I liked that it went on in the morning and was ready at suppertime with just a few minutes to thicken it right before we ate."
—TASTYCOOK1, TASTEOFHOME.COM

BANDITO CHILI DOGS

These deluxe chili dogs are a surefire hit at family functions. Adults and children alike love the cheesy chili sauce, and the toppings are fun!

—Marion Lowery, Medford, OR

PREP: 15 MIN. • **COOK:** 4 HOURS • **MAKES:** 10 SERVINGS

1 pkg. (1 lb.) hot dogs
2 cans (15 oz. each) chili without beans
1 can (10¾ oz.) condensed cheddar cheese soup, undiluted
1 can (4 oz.) chopped green chiles
10 hot dog buns, split
1 medium onion, chopped
1 to 2 cups corn chips, coarsely crushed
1 cup shredded cheddar cheese

1. Place hot dogs in a 3-qt. slow cooker. In a large bowl, combine chili, soup and green chiles; pour over hot dogs. Cover and cook on low for 4-5 hours.

2. Serve hot dogs in buns; top with chili mixture, onion, corn chips and cheese.

1 CHILI DOG 450 cal., 23g fat (10g sat. fat), 53mg chol., 1442mg sod., 43g carb. (6g sugars, 3g fiber), 19g pro.

READER REVIEW
"Perfect! Easy to cook and tastes yummy. My kids just love this and ask me to make it frequently. One of their favorite meals."
—MARYNICHOLE, TASTEOFHOME.COM

TILAPIA FLORENTINE FOIL PACKETS

I love fish and serving healthy food to my family. This is a winner in my house!
—*Shanna Belz, Prineville, OR*

PREP: 30 MIN. • **GRILL:** 15 MIN. • **MAKES:** 4 SERVINGS

12 **cups fresh baby spinach**
1   **Tbsp. butter**
1   **Tbsp. extra virgin olive oil, divided**
4   **tilapia fillets (6 oz. each)**
½   **tsp. salt**
¼   **tsp. pepper**
½   **large sweet or red onion, thinly sliced**
2   **Tbsp. fresh lemon juice**
2   **garlic cloves, minced**
    Lemon wedges, optional

1. Prepare grill for medium-high heat or preheat oven to 475°. In a large skillet, cook spinach in butter and 1 tsp. oil over medium-high heat until wilted, 8-10 minutes.
2. Divide spinach among four 18x12-in. pieces of heavy-duty nonstick foil, placing food on dull side of foil. Place tilapia on top of spinach; sprinkle with salt and pepper. Top with onion, lemon juice, garlic and remaining 2 tsp. olive oil. Fold foil around mixture, sealing tightly.
3. Place packets on grill or on a baking pan in oven. Cook until fish just begins to flake easily with a fork, 12-15 minutes. Open packets carefully to allow steam to escape. Serve with lemon wedges if desired.

1 PACKET 233 cal., 8g fat (3g sat. fat), 90mg chol., 453mg sod., 8g carb. (3g sugars, 2g fiber), 35g pro. **DIABETIC EXCHANGES** 5 lean meat, 1 vegetable, 1 fat.

5i SLOW-COOKER KALUA PORK & CABBAGE

My slow-cooker pork has four ingredients and takes less than 10 minutes to prep. The result tastes just like the luscious slow-roasted *kalua* pork that's served in Hawaii.
—Rholinelle DeTorres, San Jose, CA

PREP: 10 MIN. • **COOK:** 9 HOURS • **MAKES:** 12 SERVINGS

7 bacon strips, divided
1 boneless pork shoulder butt roast (3 to 4 lbs.), well trimmed
1 Tbsp. coarse sea salt
1 medium head cabbage (about 2 lbs.), coarsely chopped

1. Line bottom of a 6-qt. slow cooker with 4 bacon strips. Sprinkle all sides of roast with salt; place in slow cooker. Arrange remaining bacon over top of roast.
2. Cook, covered, on low for 8-10 hours or until pork is tender. Add cabbage, spreading cabbage around roast. Cook, covered, 1-1¼ hours longer or until cabbage is tender.
3. Remove pork to a serving bowl; shred pork with 2 forks. Using a slotted spoon, add cabbage to pork and toss to combine. If desired, skim fat from some of the cooking juices; stir juices into pork mixture or serve on the side.
1 CUP 227 cal., 13g fat (5g sat. fat), 72mg chol., 622mg sod., 4g carb. (2g sugars, 2g fiber), 22g pro.

DID YOU KNOW?

The kalua pork name comes from this dish's Hawaiian roots. This type of pork is typically served at luaus and other gatherings in Hawaii, where it's also known as kalua pig. Kalua refers to the style of cooking in an underground oven of sorts called an imu.

ONE-POT DINNER

Everyone comes back for seconds when I serve this well-seasoned skillet supper. I like the fact that it's on the table in just 30 minutes.
—*Bonnie Morrow, Spencerport, NY*

TAKES: 30 MIN. • **MAKES:** 5 SERVINGS

½ lb. ground beef
1 medium onion, chopped
1 cup chopped celery
¾ cup chopped green pepper
2 tsp. Worcestershire sauce
1 tsp. salt, optional
½ tsp. dried basil
¼ tsp. pepper
2 cups uncooked medium egg noodles
1 can (16 oz.) kidney beans, rinsed and drained
1 can (14½ oz.) stewed tomatoes
¾ cup water
1 beef bouillon cube

1. In a large saucepan or skillet, cook beef, onion, celery and green pepper over medium heat until vegetables are crisp-tender and meat is no longer pink; drain. Add Worcestershire sauce, salt if desired, basil and pepper. Stir in noodles, beans, tomatoes, water and bouillon.
2. Bring to a boil. Reduce heat; cover and simmer until noodles are tender, about 20 minutes, stirring occasionally.
1 CUP 263 cal., 6g fat (2g sat. fat), 41mg chol., 535mg sod., 36g carb. (8g sugars, 7g fiber), 17g pro.

READER REVIEW
"Very unique recipe! It's a mix of a stew and chili with noodles. This is an original dish with a delicious mix of ingredients."
—JENNIFER084, TASTEOFHOME.COM

PRESSURE-COOKER RIGATONI WITH SAUSAGE & PEAS

With a tomatoey meat sauce and tangy goat cheese, this weeknight wonder is my version of comfort food. You want to have bowl after bowl.

—Lizzie Munro, Brooklyn, NY

PREP: 10 MIN. • **COOK:** 20 MIN. • **MAKES:** 6 SERVINGS

1 lb. bulk Italian sausage
4 garlic cloves, minced
¼ cup tomato paste
12 oz. uncooked rigatoni or large tube pasta
1½ cups frozen peas
1 can (28 oz.) crushed tomatoes
½ tsp. dried basil
¼ to ½ tsp. crushed red pepper flakes
4 cups water
½ cup heavy whipping cream
½ cup crumbled goat or feta cheese
  Thinly sliced fresh basil, optional

1. Select saute or browning setting on a 6-qt. electric pressure cooker; adjust for medium heat. Cook sausage until no longer pink, 4-6 minutes, breaking into crumbles. Add garlic; cook 1 minute longer. Add tomato paste; cook and stir until meat is coated, 1-2 minutes. Press cancel. Stir in next 5 ingredients; pour in water.

2. Lock the lid; close pressure-release valve. Adjust to pressure-cook on low for 6 minutes. Quick-release pressure. Stir in cream; heat through. Top with cheese and, if desired, fresh basil.

1⅔ CUPS 563 cal., 28g fat (12g sat. fat), 75mg chol., 802mg sod., 60g carb. (11g sugars, 7g fiber), 23g pro.

SEAFOOD CIOPPINO

If you're looking for a great seafood recipe for your slow cooker, this classic fish stew is just the ticket. It's brimming with clams, crab, fish and shrimp, and it is fancy enough to be an elegant meal.

—*Lisa Moriarty, Wilton, NH*

PREP: 20 MIN. • **COOK:** 4½ HOURS • **MAKES:** 8 SERVINGS (2½ QT.)

1 can (28 oz.) diced
  tomatoes, undrained
2 medium onions, chopped
3 celery ribs, chopped
1 bottle (8 oz.) clam juice
1 can (6 oz.) tomato paste
½ cup white wine or ½ cup
  vegetable broth
5 garlic cloves, minced
1 Tbsp. red wine vinegar
1 Tbsp. olive oil
1 to 2 tsp. Italian seasoning
1 bay leaf
½ tsp. sugar
1 lb. haddock fillets, cut
  into 1-in. pieces
1 lb. uncooked shrimp
  (41-50 per lb.), peeled and
  deveined
1 can (6 oz.) chopped clams,
  undrained
1 can (6 oz.) lump crabmeat,
  drained
2 Tbsp. minced fresh parsley

1. In a 4- or 5-qt. slow cooker, combine first 12 ingredients. Cook, covered, on low for 4-5 hours.

2. Stir in seafood. Cook, covered, until fish just begins to flake easily with a fork and shrimp turn pink, 20-30 minutes longer.

3. Remove bay leaf. Stir in parsley.

1¼ CUPS 205 cal., 3g fat (1g sat. fat), 125mg chol., 483mg sod., 15g carb. (8g sugars, 3g fiber), 29g pro. **DIABETIC EXCHANGES** 3 lean meat, 2 vegetable.

EASY DOES IT

This is a flexible recipe— so you can add or replace foods as your taste, budget and time allow. For spicy heat, include crushed red pepper flakes or hot sauce. In place of haddock, use cod, tilapia or another firm white fish. Add other types of seafood, such as lobster, scallops, mussels or octopus. When tomatoes are in season, throw in a few diced ripe plum tomatoes. Also consider diced carrots or sliced fennel. Lastly, a splash of dry vermouth or red wine would be a classic complement for tomatoes and seafood.

LENTIL & CHICKEN SAUSAGE STEW

This hearty and healthy stew will warm your family right down to their toes! Serve with cornbread or rolls to soak up every last morsel.
—*Jan Valdez, Chicago, IL*

PREP: 15 MIN. • **COOK:** 8 HOURS • **MAKES:** 6 SERVINGS. (2¼ QT.)

1 carton (32 oz.) reduced-sodium chicken broth
1 can (28 oz.) diced tomatoes, undrained
3 fully cooked spicy chicken sausage links (3 oz. each), cut into ½-in. slices
1 cup dried lentils, rinsed
1 medium onion, chopped
1 medium carrot, chopped
1 celery rib, chopped
2 garlic cloves, minced
½ tsp. dried thyme

In a 4- or 5-qt. slow cooker, combine all ingredients. Cover and cook on low for 8-10 hours or until lentils are tender.
1½ CUPS 231 cal., 4g fat (1g sat. fat), 33mg chol., 803mg sod., 31g carb. (8g sugars, 13g fiber), 19g pro. **DIABETIC EXCHANGES** 2 vegetable, 2 lean meat, 1 starch.

⑤ SHREDDED PORK WITH BEANS

A friend gave me this recipe, which my sons say is a keeper. For a change of pace, spoon the tasty filling into soft tortillas.
—*Sarah Johnston, Lincoln, NE*

PREP: 20 MIN. • **COOK:** 8 HOURS • **MAKES:** 12 SERVINGS

3 lbs. pork tenderloins, cut into 3-in. lengths
2 cans (15 oz. each) black beans, rinsed and drained
1 jar (24 oz.) picante sauce
Hot cooked rice, optional

In a 5-qt. slow cooker, place pork, beans and picante sauce. Cover and cook on low for 8 hours or until pork is tender. Shred pork; return to slow cooker. Serve with rice if desired.
1 CUP 207 cal., 4g fat (1g sat. fat), 64mg chol., 595mg sod., 14g carb. (2g sugars, 3g fiber), 26g pro. **DIABETIC EXCHANGES** 3 lean meat, 1 starch.

LENTIL & CHICKEN
SAUSAGE STEW

MEDITERRANEAN CHICKEN ORZO

Orzo pasta with chicken, olives and herbes de Provence has the bright flavors of Mediterranean cuisine. Here's a bonus: Leftovers reheat well.

—*Thomas Faglon, Somerset, NJ*

PREP: 15 MIN. • **COOK:** 4 HOURS • **MAKES:** 6 SERVINGS

1½ lbs. boneless skinless chicken thighs, cut into 1-in. pieces
2 cups reduced-sodium chicken broth
2 medium tomatoes, finely chopped
1 cup sliced pitted green olives
1 cup sliced pitted ripe olives
1 large carrot, finely chopped
1 small red onion, finely chopped
1 Tbsp. grated lemon zest
3 Tbsp. lemon juice
2 Tbsp. butter
1 Tbsp. herbes de Provence
1 cup uncooked orzo pasta

In a 3- or 4-qt. slow cooker, combine first 11 ingredients. Cook, covered, on low until chicken, pasta and vegetables are tender, 4-5 hours, adding orzo during last 30 minutes of cooking.

1⅓ CUPS 415 cal., 19g fat (5g sat. fat), 86mg chol., 941mg sod., 33g carb. (4g sugars, 3g fiber), 27g pro.

TEST KITCHEN TIP

Herbes de Provence is a mixture of dried herbs associated with France's Provence region. It is available in the spice aisle. Use herbes de Provence to flavor mild main ingredients, such as chicken, fish and vegetables.

CHICKEN SOFT TACOS

My family loves these tacos. The chicken cooks in the slow cooker, so it's convenient to throw together before I leave for work. Then we just roll it up in tortillas with the remaining ingredients and dinner's ready in minutes.
—*Cheryl Newendorp, Pella, IA*

PREP: 30 MIN. • **COOK:** 5 HOURS • **MAKES:** 5 SERVINGS

1 broiler/fryer chicken
  (3½ lbs.), cut up and
  skin removed
1 can (8 oz.) tomato sauce
1 can (4 oz.) chopped
  green chiles
⅓ cup chopped onion
2 Tbsp. chili powder
2 Tbsp. Worcestershire
  sauce
¼ tsp. garlic powder
10 flour tortillas (8 in.),
  warmed
1¼ cups shredded
  cheddar cheese
1¼ cups salsa
1¼ cups shredded lettuce
1 large tomato, chopped
  Sour cream, optional

1. Place chicken pieces in a 4-qt. slow cooker. In a small bowl, combine tomato sauce, green chiles, onion, chili powder, Worcestershire sauce and garlic powder; pour over chicken. Cover and cook on low until chicken is tender and juices run clear, 5-6 hours.

2. Remove chicken. Shred meat with 2 forks and return to slow cooker; heat through. Spoon ½ cup chicken mixture down center of each tortilla. Top with cheese, salsa, lettuce, tomato and, if desired, sour cream; roll up.

2 TACOS 749 cal., 29g fat (13g sat. fat), 157mg chol., 1454mg sod., 64g carb. (6g sugars, 5g fiber), 52g pro.

PRESSURE-COOKER KIELBASA & CABBAGE

My grandmother was Polish and made this dish often. It's an excellent one-pot meal. We enjoy our veggies soft, but if you like them a bit crisp, cook them for 5 minutes. Also, you can sub any precooked sausage for the kielbasa.
—*Beverly Dolfini, Surprise, AZ*

PREP: 25 MIN. • **COOK:** 10 MIN. • **MAKES:** 4 SERVINGS

- 1 pkg. (14 oz.) smoked turkey kielbasa, sliced
- 1 small head cabbage, cut into 1-in. pieces
- 4 medium carrots, sliced
- 4 small red potatoes, peeled and halved
- 1 cup vegetable broth
- 1 small onion, chopped
- ½ cup sauerkraut, rinsed and well drained
- 3 Tbsp. butter, cubed
- ½ tsp. garlic powder
- ¼ tsp. salt

Place all ingredients in a 6-qt. electric pressure cooker. Lock lid; close pressure-release valve. Adjust to pressure-cook on high for 6 minutes. Quick-release pressure.

1 SERVING 318 cal., 14g fat (7g sat. fat), 85mg chol., 1552mg sod., 29g carb. (12g sugars, 8g fiber), 20g pro.

READER REVIEW
"This far exceeded my expectations. It's so good, so perfect. Divine! This will definitely join my rotation."
—MARTIFERNANDEZ, TASTEOFHOME.COM

⑤ ❄ SAVORY BEER PORK CHOPS

These tender chops cooked in a savory sauce are perfect for a hectic weeknight because they're so easy to prep. Try them with hot buttery noodles.

—Jana Christian, Farson, WY

TAKES: 20 MIN. • **MAKES:** 4 SERVINGS

4 **boneless pork loin chops (4 oz. each)**
½ **tsp. salt**
½ **tsp. pepper**
1 **Tbsp. canola oil**
3 **Tbsp. ketchup**
2 **Tbsp. brown sugar**
¾ **cup beer or nonalcoholic beer**

1. Sprinkle pork chops with salt and pepper. In a large skillet, heat oil over medium heat; brown chops on both sides.
2. Mix ketchup, brown sugar and beer; pour over chops. Bring to a boil. Reduce heat; simmer, uncovered, 4-6 minutes or until a thermometer inserted in pork reads 145°. Let stand 5 minutes before serving.

FREEZE OPTION Place pork chops in freezer containers; top with sauce. Cool and freeze. To use, partially thaw in refrigerator overnight. Heat through in a covered saucepan, gently stirring sauce; add water if necessary.

1 PORK CHOP 239 cal., 10g fat (3g sat. fat), 55mg chol., 472mg sod., 11g carb. (11g sugars, 0 fiber), 22g pro. **DIABETIC EXCHANGES** 3 lean meat, 1 fat, ½ starch.

❄ FAMILY-FAVORITE ITALIAN BEEF SANDWICHES

With only a few ingredients, this roast beef is a snap to throw together. And after cooking all day, the meat is wonderfully tender.
—*Lauren Adamson, Layton, UT*

PREP: 10 MIN. • **COOK:** 8 HOURS • **MAKES:** 12 SERVINGS

1 jar (16 oz.) sliced pepperoncini, undrained
1 can (14½ oz.) diced tomatoes, undrained
1 medium onion, chopped
½ cup water
2 pkg. Italian salad dressing mix
1 tsp. dried oregano
½ tsp. garlic powder
1 beef rump roast or bottom round roast (3 to 4 lbs.)
12 Italian rolls, split

1. In a bowl, mix first 7 ingredients. Place roast in a 5- or 6-qt. slow cooker. Pour pepperoncini mixture over top. Cook, covered, on low for 8-10 hours or until meat is tender.

2. Remove roast; cool slightly. Skim fat from cooking juices. Shred beef with 2 forks. Return beef and cooking juices to slow cooker; heat through. Serve on rolls.

PREP & FREEZE OPTION In a large freezer container, combine first 7 ingredients. Add roast; cover container and freeze. To use, place filled container in refrigerator for 48 hours or until roast is completely thawed. Cook and serve as directed.

FREEZE OPTION Freeze cooled, cooked beef mixture in freezer containers. To use, partially thaw in refrigerator overnight. Heat through in a saucepan, stirring occasionally; add water if necessary.

1 SANDWICH 278 cal., 7g fat (2g sat. fat), 67mg chol., 735mg sod., 24g carb. (3g sugars, 2g fiber), 26g pro. **DIABETIC EXCHANGES** 3 lean meat, 2 starch.

SLOW-COOKER MUSHROOM CHICKEN & PEAS

Some amazingly fresh mushrooms I found at our local farmers market inspired this recipe. When you start with the best ingredients, you can't go wrong.

—*Jenn Tidwell, Fair Oaks, CA*

PREP: 10 MIN. • **COOK:** 3 HOURS 10 MIN. • **MAKES:** 4 SERVINGS

- 4 **boneless skinless chicken breast halves (6 oz. each)**
- 1 **envelope onion mushroom soup mix**
- 1 **cup water**
- ½ **lb. sliced baby portobello mushrooms**
- 1 **medium onion, chopped**
- 4 **garlic cloves, minced**
- 2 **cups frozen peas, thawed**

1. Place chicken in a 3-qt. slow cooker. Sprinkle with soup mix, pressing to help seasonings adhere. Add water, mushrooms, onion and garlic.

2. Cook, covered, on low 3-4 hours or until chicken is tender (a thermometer inserted in chicken should read at least 165°). Stir in peas; cook, covered, 10 minutes longer or until heated through.

1 CHICKEN BREAST HALF WITH ¾ CUP VEGETABLE MIXTURE
292 cal., 5g fat (1g sat. fat), 94mg chol., 566mg sod., 20g carb. (7g sugars, 5g fiber), 41g pro. **DIABETIC EXCHANGES** 5 lean meat, 1 starch, 1 vegetable.

READER REVIEW
"Delicious. If you have it, use a cup of white wine—not water. I also used 16 oz. of sliced mushrooms. This made plenty of juice. I served it with garlic mashed potatoes. My company loved it."

—BUTTERFLYBIRDS, TASTEOFHOME.COM

ONE-PAN CHICKEN RICE CURRY

I've been loving the subtle spice from curry lately, so I incorporated it into this saucy chicken and rice dish. It's a one-pan meal that's become a go-to dinnertime favorite.
—*Mary Lou Timpson, Colorado City, AZ*

TAKES: 30 MIN. • **MAKES:** 4 SERVINGS

- 2 Tbsp. butter, divided
- 1 medium onion, halved and thinly sliced
- 2 Tbsp. all-purpose flour
- 3 tsp. curry powder
- ½ tsp. salt
- ½ tsp. pepper
- 1 lb. boneless skinless chicken breasts, cut into 1-in. pieces
- 1 can (14½ oz.) reduced-sodium chicken broth
- 1 cup uncooked instant rice
  Chopped fresh cilantro leaves, optional

1. In a large nonstick skillet, heat 1 Tbsp. butter over medium-high heat; saute onion for 3-5 minutes or until tender and lightly browned. Remove from pan.

2. In a bowl, mix flour and seasonings; toss with chicken. In same skillet, heat remaining butter over medium-high heat. Add chicken; cook for 4-6 minutes or just until no longer pink, turning occasionally.

3. Stir in broth and onion; bring to a boil. Stir in rice. Remove from heat; let stand, covered, 5 minutes (mixture will be saucy). If desired, sprinkle with cilantro.

1 CUP 300 cal., 9g fat (4g sat. fat), 78mg chol., 658mg sod., 27g carb. (2g sugars, 2g fiber), 27g pro. **DIABETIC EXCHANGES** 3 lean meat, 2 starch, 1½ fat.

BEEF & BEANS

This deliciously spicy steak and beans over rice will have family and friends asking for more. It's a favorite in my recipe collection.

—*Marie Leamon, Bethesda, MD*

PREP: 10 MIN. • **COOK:** 6½ HOURS • **MAKES:** 8 SERVINGS

1½ lbs. boneless round steak
1 Tbsp. prepared mustard
1 Tbsp. chili powder
½ tsp. salt
¼ tsp. pepper
1 garlic clove, minced
2 cans (14½ oz. each) diced tomatoes, undrained
1 medium onion, chopped
1 tsp. beef bouillon granules
1 can (16 oz.) kidney beans, rinsed and drained
Hot cooked rice

Cut steak into thin strips. Combine mustard, chili powder, salt, pepper and garlic in a bowl; add steak and toss to coat. Transfer to a 3-qt. slow cooker; add tomatoes, onion and bouillon. Cover and cook on low for 6-8 hours. Stir in beans; cook 30 minutes longer. Serve over rice.

1 CUP 185 cal., 3g fat (1g sat. fat), 47mg chol., 584mg sod., 16g carb. (5g sugars, 5g fiber), 24g pro. **DIABETIC EXCHANGES** 2 lean meat, 1 starch, 1 vegetable.

EASY DOES IT

You can easily customize this round steak by sneaking in a few more of your favorite vegetables. Consider doubling the onion, adding a julienned bell pepper, or tossing in ½ lb. sliced baby portobello mushrooms.

PRESSURE-COOKER SIMPLE POACHED SALMON

I love this recipe because it's healthy and almost effortless. The salmon always cooks to perfection and is ready in hardly any time!

—*Erin Chilcoat, Central Islip, NY*

PREP: 10 MIN. • **COOK:** 5 MIN. • **MAKES:** 4 SERVINGS

2   cups water
1   cup white wine
1   medium onion, sliced
1   celery rib, sliced
1   medium carrot, sliced
2   Tbsp. lemon juice
3   fresh thyme sprigs
1   fresh rosemary sprig
1   bay leaf
½   tsp. salt
¼   tsp. pepper
4   salmon fillets (1¼ in. thick and 6 oz. each)
    Lemon wedges

1. Combine first 11 ingredients in a 6-qt. electric pressure cooker; top with salmon. Lock lid; close pressure-release valve. Adjust to pressure-cook on high for 3 minutes. Quick-release pressure. A thermometer inserted in fish should read at least 145°.

2. Remove fish from pressure cooker. Serve warm or cold with lemon wedges.

1 SALMON FILLET 270 cal., 16g fat (3g sat. fat), 85mg chol., 115mg sod., 0 carb. (0 sugars, 0 fiber), 29g pro. **DIABETIC EXCHANGES** 4 lean meat.

DID YOU KNOW?

You can tell whether salmon is wild-caught or farm-raised depending on its appearance. Wild-caught is more lean, red in color and has thin stripes of fat, while farm-raised is thicker, orange in color and has large stripes of fat.

GERMAN CHOCOLATE
DUMP CAKE, PAGE 236

LAZY-DAY DESSERTS

CHERRY PUDDING CAKE

A cross between a cake and a cobbler, this cherry dessert is awesome. Add it to your list of trusty potluck recipes, because this one is sure to go fast.
—*Brenda Parker, Kalamazoo, MI*

PREP: 10 MIN. • **BAKE:** 40 MIN. • **MAKES:** 12 SERVINGS

2 cups all-purpose flour
2½ cups sugar, divided
4 tsp. baking powder
1 cup 2% milk
2 Tbsp. canola oil
2 cans (14½ oz. each) water-packed pitted tart red cherries, well drained
⅛ tsp. almond extract
Optional: Whipped cream or ice cream

1. In a bowl, combine flour, 1 cup sugar, baking powder, milk and oil; pour into a greased shallow 3-qt. baking dish. In a bowl, combine cherries, extract and remaining 1½ cups sugar; spoon over batter.
2. Bake at 375° for 40-45 minutes or until a toothpick inserted in the cake portion comes out clean. Serve warm, with whipped cream or ice cream if desired.
1 SERVING 296 cal., 3g fat (1g sat. fat), 3mg chol., 147mg sod., 65g carb. (48g sugars, 1g fiber), 3g pro.

FRESH PEACH COBBLER

I use the delicious peaches only available in late summer to make this classic dessert. I especially enjoy the nutmeg flavor.
—*Pat Kinghorn, Morrill, NE*

PREP: 10 MIN. • **BAKE:** 45 MIN. • **MAKES:** 8 SERVINGS

4 large peaches, peeled and sliced
1½ cups sugar, divided
½ cup butter, melted
1 cup all-purpose flour
2 tsp. baking powder
¼ tsp. salt
Dash ground nutmeg
¾ cup milk

Combine peaches and ¾ cup sugar; set aside. Pour butter into an 8-in. square baking dish. In a small bowl, combine flour, baking powder, salt, nutmeg and remaining sugar; stir in milk just until combined. Pour over butter. Top with peach mixture. Bake at 375° for 45-50 minutes or until golden brown.
1 SERVING 327 cal., 12g fat (8g sat. fat), 34mg chol., 301mg sod., 53g carb. (40g sugars, 1g fiber), 3g pro.

CHERRY PUDDING CAKE

NEW ENGLAND INDIAN PUDDING

This recipe was inspired by traditional New England Indian pudding. My version is made in the slow cooker instead of being baked for hours in the oven. For a milder molasses flavor, cut the amount to ⅓ cup.

—*Susan Bickta, Kutztown, PA*

PREP: 15 MIN. • **COOK:** 3½ HOURS • **MAKES:** 8 SERVINGS

1 pkg. (8½ oz.) cornbread/
  muffin mix
1 pkg. (3.4 oz.) instant
  butterscotch pudding mix
4 cups whole milk
3 large eggs, room
  temperature, lightly
  beaten
½ cup molasses
1 tsp. ground cinnamon
¼ tsp. ground cloves
¼ tsp. ground ginger
  Optional: Vanilla ice cream
  or sweetened whipped
  cream

1. In a large bowl, whisk cornbread mix, pudding mix and milk until blended. Add eggs, molasses and spices; whisk until combined. Transfer to a greased 4- or 5-qt. slow cooker. Cover and cook on high for 1 hour.

2. Reduce heat to low. Stir pudding, making sure to scrape side of slow cooker well. Cover and cook until very thick, 2½-3 hours longer, stirring once per hour. Serve warm, with ice cream or whipped cream if desired.

⅔ CUP 330 cal., 9g fat (4g sat. fat), 83mg chol., 526mg sod., 51g carb. (36g sugars, 2g fiber), 8g pro.

TEST KITCHEN TIP

This method is a little different from other slow-cooker recipes. You really do have to make time to stir it periodically, or the edges will get too dark.

CRANBERRY-APPLE NUT CRUNCH

My mother gave me the recipe for this dessert, which I think is especially pretty and very appropriate for fall. I updated the recipe to use instant oatmeal to make it even easier.
—*Joyce Sheets, Lafayette, IN*

PREP: 15 MIN. • **BAKE:** 50 MIN. • **MAKES:** 8 SERVINGS

3 **cups chopped peeled apples**
2 **cups fresh or frozen cranberries**
3 **Tbsp. all-purpose flour**
1 **cup sugar**

TOPPING
3 **packets (1.51 oz. each) instant oatmeal with cinnamon and spice**
¾ **cup chopped pecans**
½ **cup all-purpose flour**
½ **cup packed brown sugar**
½ **cup butter, melted**
   Whole cranberries for garnish
   Vanilla ice cream, optional

In a large bowl, combine first 4 ingredients and mix well. Place in a 2-qt. baking dish. For topping, combine oatmeal, pecans, flour, sugar and butter in another bowl. Mix well; spoon evenly over fruit mixture. Bake, uncovered, at 350° for 50-60 minutes or until fruit is bubbly and tender. Garnish with cranberries. Serve warm with ice cream if desired.

1 CUP 422 cal., 20g fat (8g sat. fat), 31mg chol., 152mg sod., 62g carb. (47g sugars, 3g fiber), 3g pro.

READER REVIEW
"I love this recipe! I doubled it and used a 9×13-in. pan. Scrumptious! It was such a hit for Thanksgiving that I made it last year and this year."
—KATHLEEN1628, TASTEOFHOME.COM

CINNAMON
SPICED APPLES

CINNAMON SPICED APPLES

If you're feeling festive, scoop some vanilla ice cream over a bowl of my cinnamon spiced apples. They're homey, aromatic and just plain heavenly.
—*Amie Powell, Knoxville, TN*

PREP: 15 MIN. • **COOK:** 3 HOURS • **MAKES:** 6 CUPS

⅓ cup sugar
¼ cup packed brown sugar
1 Tbsp. cornstarch
3 tsp. ground cinnamon
⅛ tsp. ground nutmeg
6 large Granny Smith apples, peeled and cut into eighths
¼ cup butter, cubed

In a small bowl, mix first 5 ingredients. Place apples in a greased 5-qt. slow cooker; add sugar mixture and toss to coat. Top with butter. Cook, covered, on low for 3-4 hours or until apples are tender, stirring halfway through cooking.

¾ CUP 181 cal., 6g fat (4g sat. fat), 15mg chol., 48mg sod., 34g carb. (29g sugars, 2g fiber), 0 pro.

ORANGE LOAF CAKE

Our state's abundant orange juice is put to excellent use in this moist cake. The citrus flavor is simply irresistible!
—*Dawn Congleton, Orlando, FL*

PREP: 15 MIN. • **BAKE:** 1 HOUR + COOLING • **MAKES:** 12 SERVINGS

1¾ cups cake flour
1 cup sugar
2 tsp. baking powder
¼ tsp. salt
½ cup canola oil
½ cup orange juice
4 egg whites
2 Tbsp. confectioners' sugar

1. In a large bowl, combine dry ingredients. Add oil and orange juice; beat until smooth. In another bowl, beat egg whites until stiff peaks form. Fold into orange juice mixture. Coat a 9x5-in. loaf pan with cooking spray; dust with flour. Pour batter into pan.

2. Bake at 350° for 1 hour or until a toothpick inserted in the center comes out clean. Cool for 10 minutes before removing from pan to wire rack to cool completely. Dust with confectioners' sugar.

1 PIECE 152 cal., 0 fat, 0 chol., 134mg sod., 35g carb., 0 fiber), 3g pro.

SLOW-COOKER SPUMONI CAKE

I created this cake for a holiday potluck one year. It has become one of my most requested desserts. If you prefer, you can use all semisweet chips instead of a mix.

—Lisa Renshaw, Kansas City, MO

PREP: 10 MIN. • **COOK:** 4 HOURS + STANDING • **MAKES:** 10 SERVINGS

3 cups cold 2% milk
1 pkg. (3.4 oz.) instant pistachio pudding mix
1 pkg. white cake mix (regular size)
¾ cup chopped maraschino cherries
1 cup white baking chips
1 cup semisweet chocolate chips
1 cup pistachios, chopped

1. In a large bowl, whisk milk and pudding mix for 2 minutes. Transfer to a greased 5-qt. slow cooker. Prepare cake mix batter according to package directions, folding cherries into batter. Pour into slow cooker.

2. Cook, covered, on low for 4 hours or until edge of cake is golden brown.

3. Remove slow-cooker insert; sprinkle cake with baking chips and chocolate chips. Let cake stand, uncovered, 10 minutes. Sprinkle with pistachios before serving.

1 SERVING 588 cal., 27g fat (9g sat. fat), 9mg chol., 594mg sod., 79g carb. (54g sugars, 3g fiber), 10g pro.

BLUEBERRY, APPLE & PINEAPPLE DUMP CAKE

I call this B.A.P. dump cake. I usually take it to our church potluck and it is the first dessert to go! Sometimes I sprinkle a little extra sugar over the nuts.

—*Mitzi Erthal, Godfrey, IL*

PREP: 10 MIN. BAKE 45 MIN. • **MAKES:** 15 SERVINGS

1 can (21 oz.) apple pie filling
1 can (8 oz.) unsweetened crushed pineapple, drained
1 pkg. (12 oz.) frozen unsweetened blueberries
½ cup sugar
1 pkg. white cake mix (regular size)
⅔ cup butter, melted
1 cup chopped walnuts
½ cup sliced almonds

1. Preheat oven to 350°. Stir pie filling and pineapple in a greased 13x9-in. baking dish until combined. Toss blueberries with sugar; spoon over pie filling mixture. Sprinkle with cake mix; drizzle with butter. Top with walnuts and almonds (do not stir).

2. Bake cake until golden brown and bubbly, 45-55 minutes. Serve warm.

⅔ CUP 332 cal., 16g fat (6g sat. fat), 22mg chol., 285mg sod., 47g carb. (28g sugars, 3g fiber), 3g pro.

EASY DOES IT

For a rich and creamy counterpoint, top this dessert with a little half-and-half cream, whipped cream or ice cream.

CHOCOLATE-PEANUT BUTTER DUMP CAKE

I am a huge fan of the chocolate-peanut butter combination. I'm also a fan of easy recipes, including dump cakes. On occasion, I've omitted the peanut butter chips and used 1½ cups semisweet chocolate chips with very tasty results.

—Lisa Varner, El Paso, TX

PREP: 15 MIN. • **BAKE:** 20 MIN. + COOLING • **MAKES:** 15 SERVINGS

1 pkg. (3.9 oz.) instant chocolate pudding mix
1¾ cups 2% milk
1 pkg. chocolate or devil's food cake mix (regular size)
6 pkg. (1½ oz. each) peanut butter cups, chopped
¾ cup peanut butter chips
¾ cup semisweet chocolate chips
½ cup chopped unsalted peanuts
Optional: Vanilla ice cream or sweetened whipped cream

1. Preheat oven to 350°. Grease a 13x9-in. baking pan. In a large bowl, combine pudding mix and milk until blended. Stir in cake mix (batter will be thick). Fold in peanut butter cups, peanut butter chips and chocolate chips. Spread into prepared pan. Sprinkle with peanuts.

2. Bake until a toothpick inserted in center comes out with moist crumbs, 20-25 minutes. Cool completely in pan on a wire rack. Serve with ice cream or whipped cream if desired.

1 PIECE 349 cal., 14g fat (6g sat. fat), 3mg chol., 373mg sod., 51g carb. (33g sugars, 3g fiber), 7g pro.

READER REVIEW

"Delicious. I had miniature peanut butter cups I'd bought at the Mennonite store that I used instead of chopping up large ones. Also, I left off the peanuts on top and instead sprinkled on a few more miniature peanut butter cups. So good!"
—GRAMMY DEBBIE, TASTEOFHOME.COM

EASY CHOCOLATE CHIP PUMPKIN BARS

🅣 EASY CHOCOLATE CHIP PUMPKIN BARS

This dessert is super easy to pull together, and the flavorful results will win you nothing but rave reviews.
—*Aimee Ransom, Hoschton, GA*

PREP: 5 MIN. • **BAKE:** 30 MIN. + COOLING • **MAKES:** 3 DOZEN

1 **pkg. spice cake mix (regular size)**
1 **can (15 oz.) solid-pack pumpkin**
2 **cups semisweet chocolate chips, divided**

1. In a large bowl, combine cake mix and pumpkin; beat on low speed for 30 seconds. Beat on medium speed for 2 minutes. Fold in 1½ cups chocolate chips. Transfer to a greased 13x9-in. baking pan.
2. Bake at 350° for 30-35 minutes or until toothpick inserted in center comes out clean. Cool completely in pan on a wire rack.
3. In a microwave, melt remaining chocolate chips; stir until smooth. Drizzle over bars. Let stand until set.
1 BAR 139 cal., 6g fat (4g sat. fat), 0 chol., 92mg sod., 23g carb. (16g sugars, 1g fiber), 1g pro.

🅣 MINISTER'S DELIGHT

A friend gave me this recipe several years ago. She said a local minister's wife fixed it every Sunday, so she named it accordingly.
—*Mary Ann Potter, Blue Springs, MO*

PREP: 5 MIN. • **COOK:** 2 HOURS • **MAKES:** 12 SERVINGS

1 **can (21 oz.) cherry or apple pie filling**
1 **pkg. yellow cake mix (regular size)**
½ **cup butter, melted**
⅓ **cup chopped walnuts, optional**

Place pie filling in a 1½-qt. slow cooker. Combine cake mix and butter (mixture will be crumbly); sprinkle over filling. Sprinkle with walnuts if desired. Cover and cook on low for 2-3 hours. Serve in bowls.
1 SERVING 304 cal., 12g fat (6g sat. fat), 20mg chol., 357mg sod., 48g carb. (31g sugars, 1g fiber), 2g pro.

BLUEBERRY PUDDING CAKE

We have many acres of blueberry bushes in the area where we live. My father-in-law has a number of them near his house, so I have an abundant supply every year. I'm always looking for new ways to use the berries. This recipe is a recent find, and it's been very popular.
—*Jan Bamford, Sedgwick, ME*

PREP: 15 MIN. • **BAKE:** 45 MIN. • **MAKES:** 9 SERVINGS

2 **cups fresh or frozen blueberries**
1 **tsp. ground cinnamon**
1 **tsp. lemon juice**
1 **cup all-purpose flour**
¾ **cup sugar**
1 **tsp. baking powder**
½ **cup 2% milk**
3 **Tbsp. butter, melted**

TOPPING
¾ **cup sugar**
1 **Tbsp. cornstarch**
1 **cup boiling water**
  Whipped cream, optional

1. Preheat oven to 350°. Toss blueberries with cinnamon and lemon juice; pour into a greased 8-in. square baking dish. In a small bowl, combine flour, sugar and baking powder; stir in milk and butter. Spoon over berries.

2. Combine sugar and cornstarch; sprinkle over batter. Slowly pour boiling water over all. Bake until a toothpick inserted into the cake portion comes out clean, 45-50 minutes. Serve warm. If desired, top with whipped cream and additional blueberries.

1 SERVING 244 cal., 4g fat (3g sat. fat), 11mg chol., 91mg sod., 51g carb. (37g sugars, 1g fiber), 2g pro.

SLOW-COOKER BANANAS FOSTER

The flavors of caramel, rum and walnut naturally complement fresh bananas in this version of a dessert classic. It's my go-to choice for any family get-together.
—Crystal Jo Bruns, Iliff, CO

PREP: 10 MIN. • **COOK:** 2 HOURS • **MAKES:** 5 SERVINGS

5 medium firm bananas
1 cup packed brown sugar
¼ cup butter, melted
¼ cup rum
1 tsp. vanilla extract
½ tsp. ground cinnamon
⅓ cup chopped walnuts
⅓ cup sweetened shredded coconut
Optional: Vanilla ice cream or sliced pound cake

1. Cut bananas in half lengthwise, then widthwise; layer in bottom of a 1½-qt. slow cooker. Combine brown sugar, butter, rum, vanilla and cinnamon; pour over bananas. Cover and cook on low until heated through, about 1½ hours.

2. Sprinkle with walnuts and coconut; cook for 30 minutes longer. Serve with ice cream or pound cake if desired.

1 SERVING 462 cal., 17g fat (8g sat. fat), 24mg chol., 99mg sod., 74g carb. (59g sugars, 4g fiber), 3g pro.

🏆 TOFFEE POKE CAKE

This toffee poke cake recipe is a favorite among my family and friends. I love making it because it is so simple.
—*Jeanette Hoffman, Oshkosh, WI*

PREP: 25 MIN. • **BAKE:** 25 MIN. + CHILLING • **MAKES:** 15 SERVINGS

1 pkg. chocolate cake mix (regular size)
1 jar (17 oz.) butterscotch-caramel ice cream topping
1 carton (12 oz.) frozen whipped topping, thawed
3 Heath candy bars (1.4 oz. each), chopped

1. Prepare and bake cake according to package directions, using a greased 13x9-in. baking pan. Cool on a wire rack.

2. Using handle of a wooden spoon, poke holes in cake. Pour ¾ cup caramel topping into holes. Spoon remaining caramel over cake. Top with whipped topping. Sprinkle with candy. Refrigerate for at least 2 hours before serving.

1 PIECE 404 cal., 16g fat (8g sat. fat), 48mg chol., 322mg sod., 60g carb. (39g sugars, 1g fiber), 4g pro.

🏆 SO-EASY FLAN CUPS

Do you enjoy ordering flan at your favorite restaurant? Now you can savor the flavor of this popular dessert in your own home. The fantastic treat is so much easier to make than you think.
—Taste of Home *Test Kitchen*

PREP: 15 MIN. • **BAKE:** 30 MIN. + CHILLING • **MAKES:** 6 SERVINGS

5 eggs
½ cup sugar
1 tsp. vanilla extract
⅛ tsp. salt
2½ cups milk
2 Tbsp. caramel ice cream topping

1. In a small bowl, whisk eggs, sugar, vanilla and salt. Gradually stir in milk. Spoon 1 tsp. caramel topping into each of 6 ungreased 6-oz. custard cups.

2. Place cups in a 13x9-in. baking dish. Pour egg mixture into cups (cups will be full). Fill baking dish with 1 in. hot water.

3. Bake, uncovered, at 350° for 30-35 minutes or until centers are almost set (mixture will jiggle). Remove custard cups from water to a wire rack; cool for 30 minutes.

4. Refrigerate for 3 hours or until thoroughly chilled. Invert and unmold onto rimmed dessert dishes.

1 CUP 208 cal., 8g fat (3g sat. fat), 191mg chol., 176mg sod., 26g carb. (26g sugars, 0 fiber), 9g pro.

TOFFEE POKE CAKE

PIG PICKIN' CAKE

This is one of my favorite cakes. It's moist and light yet so satisfying. I've been adapting it for years and now it's almost guilt-free.

—*Pam Sjolund, Columbia, SC*

PREP: 15 MIN. • **BAKE:** 25 MIN. + CHILLING • **MAKES:** 15 SERVINGS

1 pkg. yellow cake mix (regular size)
1 can (11 oz.) mandarin oranges, undrained
4 large egg whites
½ cup unsweetened applesauce

TOPPING
1 can (20 oz.) crushed pineapple, undrained
1 pkg. (1 oz.) sugar-free instant vanilla pudding mix
1 carton (8 oz.) reduced-fat whipped topping

1. In a large bowl, beat cake mix, oranges, egg whites and applesauce on low speed for 2 minutes. Pour into a 13x9-in. baking dish coated with cooking spray.

2. Bake at 350° for 25-30 minutes or until a toothpick inserted in center comes out clean. Cool on a wire rack.

3. In a bowl, combine pineapple and pudding mix. Fold in whipped topping just until blended. Spread over cake. Refrigerate for at least 1 hour before serving.

1 PIECE 218 cal., 3g fat (2g sat. fat), 0 chol., 338mg sod., 47g carb. (27g sugars, 1g fiber), 2g pro.

READER REVIEW

"My husband's Uncle Wally introduced us to Pig Pickin' Cake over 30 years ago. He explained that it's the traditional dish brought to a pig picking—a neighborhood event that follows a pig roast. After the pig is roasted, the women get together to pick and shred the leftover meat for making traditional Carolina BBQ. I have made this as a sheet cake, 2-layer cake, cupcakes, and in a springform pan, cut into 3 layers. Always delicious, and one of my very favorite desserts!"
—LEEBICK, TASTEOFHOME.COM

APPLE CORNBREAD CRISP

With its hearty ingredients and quick prep time, this warm apple crisp makes a smart dessert for any fall night. It reminds me of the recipe my grandmother would serve after our big family seafood dinners. It's absolutely wonderful topped with ice cream.
—*Julie Peterson, Crofton, MD*

PREP: 10 MIN. • **BAKE:** 30 MIN. • **MAKES:** 6 SERVINGS

4 **cups sliced peeled tart apples (4-5 medium)**
¾ **cup packed brown sugar, divided**
1 **pkg. (8½ oz.) cornbread/ muffin mix**
½ **cup quick-cooking oats**
1 **tsp. ground cinnamon (or to taste)**
5 **Tbsp. cold butter, cubed**

1. Preheat oven to 350°. Stir together apples and ¼ cup brown sugar. In another bowl, combine cornbread mix, oats, cinnamon and remaining brown sugar. Cut in butter until crumbly.

2. Add ½ cup cornbread mixture to apples. Transfer to a greased 8-in. square baking dish. Sprinkle remaining cornbread mixture over top. Bake until filling is bubbly and topping is golden brown, 30-35 minutes. Serve warm.

1 SERVING 421 cal., 15g fat (7g sat. fat), 26mg chol., 413mg sod., 70g carb. (43g sugars, 5g fiber), 4g pro.

STRAWBERRY CHEESECAKE TRIFLE

For a dessert that looks as great as it tastes, this one can't be beat! Layers of rich pound cake, luscious cream and sweet strawberries make this treat very inviting.

—*Marnie Stoughton, Glenburnie, ON*

PREP: 25 MIN. + CHILLING • **MAKES:** 16 SERVINGS

2 pints fresh strawberries, sliced
1 cup sugar, divided
2 pkg. (8 oz. each) cream cheese, softened
3 Tbsp. orange juice
3 cups heavy whipping cream, whipped
1 loaf (10¾ oz.) frozen pound cake, thawed and cut into ½-in. cubes
3 oz. semisweet chocolate, grated
Optional: Chocolate curls and additional sliced strawberries

1. In a bowl, toss strawberries with ½ cup sugar; set aside.
2. In another bowl, beat cream cheese, orange juice and remaining sugar until smooth. Fold in whipped cream; set aside.
3. Drain strawberries, reserving juice; set berries aside. Gently toss cake cubes with reserved juice. Place half the cake in a 4-qt. trifle dish or serving bowl. Top with a third of cream cheese mixture, half the strawberries and half the grated chocolate. Repeat layers. Top with remaining cream cheese mixture. Garnish with chocolate curls and strawberries if desired. Cover and refrigerate for at least 4 hours.

1 CUP 344 cal., 25g fat (15g sat. fat), 104mg chol., 129mg sod., 28g carb. (22g sugars, 1g fiber), 4g pro.

READER REVIEW

"I made this as a dessert for a cookout we hosted. Everyone loved it, and several people asked for the recipe. This was so easy to make, and the final result looked beautiful and tasted great!"
—CHERSTAD, TASTEOFHOME.COM

GERMAN CHOCOLATE DUMP CAKE

We make this for Sunday lunches when the whole family gets together. The cream cheese topping is so good that it doesn't need frosting.

—*Donna Holdbrooks, Waco, GA*

PREP: 15 MIN. • **BAKE:** 35 MIN. + COOLING • **MAKES:** 15 SERVINGS

1 cup sweetened shredded coconut
1½ cups chopped toasted pecans, divided
1 pkg. devil's food cake mix (regular size)
8 oz. cream cheese, softened
½ cup butter, melted
2 tsp. vanilla extract
2 cups confectioners' sugar
½ cup semisweet chocolate chips

1. Preheat oven to 350°. Grease a 13x9-in. baking pan.
2. Sprinkle coconut and 1 cup pecans into baking pan. Prepare cake mix according to package directions. Pour batter into prepared pan.
3. In a large bowl, beat cream cheese, butter and vanilla until smooth; beat in confectioners' sugar. Stir in chocolate chips and remaining ½ cup pecans. Spoon over batter. Cut through batter with a knife to swirl. Bake until a toothpick inserted in center comes out clean, 35-40 minutes. Cool completely in pan on a wire rack.

1 PIECE 479 cal., 30g fat (12g sat. fat), 69mg chol., 389mg sod., 50g carb. (36g sugars, 2g fiber), 5g pro.

🔟 ❄ STRAWBERRY LEMONADE FREEZER PIE

Three simple ingredients mixed together and spread into a graham cracker crust make magic while your freezer does all the work. Prep this pie ahead and freeze it overnight or even longer. Feel free to vary the fruit if you'd like!

—*Debbie Glasscock, Conway, AR*

PREP: 15 MIN. + FREEZING • **MAKES:** 8 SERVINGS

1 **container (23.2 oz.) frozen sweetened sliced strawberries, thawed (2½ cups thawed)**
1 **pkg. (3.4 oz.) instant lemon pudding mix**
1 **carton (8 oz.) frozen whipped topping, thawed**
1 **graham cracker crust (9 in.)**
  Optional: Additional whipped topping and fresh strawberries

1. In a large bowl, combine strawberries (with juices) and pudding mix; let stand until slightly thickened, about 5 minutes. Fold in whipped topping. Spread into crust.

2. Freeze at least 8 hours or overnight. Let stand 5-10 minutes before serving. If desired, serve with additional whipped topping and fresh strawberries.

1 PIECE 306 cal., 10g fat (6g sat. fat), 0 chol., 273mg sod., 51g carb. (45g sugars, 2g fiber), 1g pro.

READER REVIEW

"This was so easy to make and delicious! I served it for a Memorial Day cookout—it was a hot day, and this was so refreshing. It looks pretty with the pieces of strawberry in it. I made my own graham cracker crust, as I prefer that over store-bought."

—PATTIEJEAN, TASTEOFHOME.COM

PINEAPPLE UPSIDE-DOWN DUMP CAKE

No matter the season, this dump cake recipe is wonderful! It works well with gluten-free and sugar-free cake mixes too.
—*Karin Gatewood, Josephine, TX*

PREP: 10 MIN. • **COOK:** 2 HOURS + STANDING • **MAKES:** 10 SERVINGS

¾ cup butter, divided
⅔ cup packed brown sugar
1 jar (6 oz.) maraschino cherries, drained
½ cup chopped pecans, toasted
1 can (20 oz.) unsweetened pineapple tidbits or crushed pineapple, undrained
1 pkg. yellow cake mix (regular size)
Vanilla ice cream, optional

1. In a microwave, melt ½ cup butter; stir in brown sugar. Spread evenly onto bottom of a greased 5-qt. slow cooker. Sprinkle with cherries and pecans; top with pineapple. Sprinkle evenly with dry cake mix. Melt remaining butter; drizzle on top.
2. Cook, covered, on high for 2 hours or until fruit mixture is bubbly. (To avoid scorching, rotate slow-cooker insert a half turn midway through cooking, lifting carefully with oven mitts.)
3. Turn off slow cooker; let stand, uncovered, for 30 minutes before serving. If desired, serve with ice cream.
NOTE To toast nuts, bake in a shallow pan in a 350° oven for 5-10 minutes or cook in a skillet over low heat until lightly browned, stirring occasionally.
½ CUP 455 cal., 22g fat (10g sat. fat), 37mg chol., 418mg sod., 66g carb. (47g sugars, 1g fiber), 3g pro.

TEST KITCHEN TIPS

• Sprinkle the cake mix in an even layer over the pineapple. If it's piled high in the center, the middle of the cake may be undercooked.

• A large slow cooker is used to keep the ingredient layers thin, which promotes even cooking.

⑤i PRESSURE-COOKER CHOCOLATE-APRICOT DUMP CAKE

Years ago, I used to prepare a dessert similar to this in the oven. Oh, it was so good. I converted the recipe to use my pressure cooker, and now we can enjoy it quickly. Try it also with white cake mix and blueberry pie filling. It's best served warm with ice cream or whipped cream.
—*Joan Hallford, North Richland Hills, TX*

PREP: 10 MIN. • **COOK:** 35 MIN. + STANDING • **MAKES:** 8 SERVINGS

1 can (21 oz.) apricot or peach pie filling
2 cups devil's food cake mix
½ cup chopped pecans, toasted
½ cup miniature semisweet chocolate chips, optional
½ cup butter, cubed
Vanilla ice cream, optional

1. Spread pie filling in bottom of a greased 1½-qt. baking dish. Sprinkle with cake mix, pecans and, if desired, chocolate chips. Dot with butter. Cover baking dish with foil.

2. Place trivet insert and 1 cup water in a 6-qt. electric pressure cooker. Fold an 18x12-in. piece of foil lengthwise into thirds, making a sling. Use sling to lower dish onto trivet. Lock lid; close pressure-release valve. Adjust to pressure-cook on high for 35 minutes. Quick-release pressure. Using foil sling, carefully remove baking dish. Let stand 10 minutes. If desired, serve warm cake with ice cream.

1 SERVING 360 cal., 18g fat (9g sat. fat), 31mg chol., 436mg sod., 49g carb. (26g sugars, 1g fiber), 2g pro.

SLOW-COOKER CINNAMON ROLL PUDDING

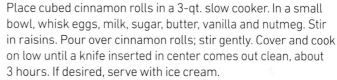

A slow cooker turns day-old cinnamon rolls into a comforting, old-fashioned dessert. It tastes wonderful topped with lemon or vanilla sauce or whipped cream.
—*Edna Hoffman, Hebron, IN*

PREP: 15 MIN. • **COOK:** 3 HOURS • **MAKES:** 6 SERVINGS

8   **cups cubed day-old unfrosted cinnamon rolls**
4   **large eggs**
2   **cups whole milk**
¼   **cup sugar**
¼   **cup butter, melted**
½   **tsp. vanilla extract**
¼   **tsp. ground nutmeg**
1   **cup raisins**
    Vanilla ice cream, optional

Place cubed cinnamon rolls in a 3-qt. slow cooker. In a small bowl, whisk eggs, milk, sugar, butter, vanilla and nutmeg. Stir in raisins. Pour over cinnamon rolls; stir gently. Cover and cook on low until a knife inserted in center comes out clean, about 3 hours. If desired, serve with ice cream.

NOTE 8 slices of cinnamon or white bread, cut into 1-in. cubes, may be substituted for the cinnamon rolls.

1 SERVING 570 cal., 27g fat (10g sat. fat), 226mg chol., 468mg sod., 72g carb. (53g sugars, 3g fiber), 13g pro.

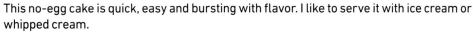

CARDAMOM PUMPKIN PUDDING CAKE

This no-egg cake is quick, easy and bursting with flavor. I like to serve it with ice cream or whipped cream.
—*J. Fleming, Almonte, ON*

PREP: 20 MIN. • **BAKE:** 25 MIN. + COOLING • **MAKES:** 9 SERVINGS

1¼ cups all-purpose flour
¾ cup sugar
2 tsp. baking soda
1¼ tsp. ground cinnamon
1 tsp. ground cardamom
¼ tsp. salt
½ cup evaporated milk
½ cup canned pumpkin
¼ cup butter, melted
1 tsp. vanilla extract
½ cup chopped pecans

TOPPING
1 cup packed brown sugar
½ tsp. ground cinnamon
1½ cups boiling water
Optional: Vanilla ice cream or sweetened whipped cream

1. Preheat oven to 350°. In a large bowl, combine the first 6 ingredients. Add milk, pumpkin, butter and vanilla; mix until blended. Stir in pecans. Transfer to a greased 9-in. square baking pan. For topping, combine brown sugar and cinnamon; sprinkle over batter. Pour water over top (do not stir).

2. Bake until a toothpick inserted in center comes out clean and liquid is bubbling around the edges, 25-30 minutes. Cool completely in pan on a wire rack. Serve with ice cream or whipped cream if desired.

1 PIECE 334 cal., 11g fat (4g sat. fat), 18mg chol., 407mg sod., 58g carb. (43g sugars, 2g fiber), 4g pro.

DID YOU KNOW?

Most of the world's canned pumpkin is produced in a Libby's factory in Morton, located near Peoria in central Illinois. Local farmers plant about 5,000 acres of pumpkins per year.

⑤ BLACK FOREST DUMP CAKE

I make a black forest cake the easy way: Dump everything into a dish and let the magic happen. To give it a cherry topping, reserve 2 Tbsp. of juice from the canned cherries and stir it into some sweetened whipped cream.
—*Meghan McDermott, Springfield, MO*

PREP: 10 MIN. • **BAKE:** 40 MIN. • **MAKES:** 12 SERVINGS

1 can (21 oz.) cherry pie filling
1 can (15 oz.) pitted dark sweet cherries, undrained
1 pkg. chocolate cake mix (regular size)
½ cup sliced almonds
¾ cup butter, cubed

1. Preheat oven to 375°. Spread pie filling into a greased 13x9-in. baking dish; top with undrained cherries. Sprinkle with cake mix and almonds. Top with cubed butter.
2. Bake until topping is set, 40-50 minutes. Serve warm or at room temperature.
1 SERVING 347 cal., 16g fat (8g sat. fat), 31mg chol., 346mg sod., 49g carb. (21g sugars, 2g fiber), 3g pro.

SLOW-COOKER LAVA CAKE

I love chocolate. Perhaps that's why this decadent slow-cooker cake has long been a family favorite. The cake can also be served cold.
—*Elizabeth Farrell, Hamilton, MT*

PREP: 15 MIN. • **COOK:** 2 HOURS + STANDING • **MAKES:** 8 SERVINGS

1 cup all-purpose flour
1 cup packed brown sugar, divided
5 Tbsp. baking cocoa, divided
2 tsp. baking powder
¼ tsp. salt
½ cup fat-free milk
2 Tbsp. canola oil
½ tsp. vanilla extract
⅛ tsp. ground cinnamon
1¼ cups hot water

1. In a large bowl, whisk flour, ½ cup brown sugar, 3 Tbsp. cocoa, baking powder and salt. In another bowl, whisk milk, oil and vanilla until blended. Add to flour mixture; stir just until moistened.
2. Spread into a 3-qt. slow cooker coated with cooking spray. In a small bowl, mix cinnamon and remaining brown sugar and cocoa; stir in hot water. Pour over batter (do not stir).
3. Cook, covered, on high for 2-2½ hours or until a toothpick inserted in cake portion comes out clean. Turn off slow cooker; let stand 15 minutes before serving.
1 SERVING 207 cal., 4g fat (0 sat. fat), 0 chol., 191mg sod., 41g carb. (28g sugars, 1g fiber), 3g pro.

BLACK FOREST DUMP CAKE

APPLE, SWEET POTATO & PECAN DUMP CAKE

This quick cake has lots of delicious apples, sweet potatoes, spices, pecans and caramel. My surprise ingredient of white cheddar cheese enhances the wonderful filling.
—*Kathy Specht, Clinton, MT*

PREP: 15 MIN. • **BAKE:** 45 MIN. + STANDING • **MAKES:** 15 SERVINGS

- 1 **can (21 oz.) apple pie filling**
- 1 **can (16 oz.) cut sweet potatoes in syrup, drained and cut into ½-in. pieces**
- 1 **tsp. ground cinnamon**
- ½ **tsp. pumpkin pie spice**
- 1 **pkg. butter pecan cake mix (regular size)**
- ¾ **cup shredded white cheddar cheese**
- ¾ **cup butter, cubed**
- ½ **cup caramel ice cream topping**
- 1 **cup chopped pecans Vanilla ice cream or sweetened whipped cream, optional**

Preheat oven to 350°. Combine pie filling, sweet potatoes, cinnamon and pie spice in a greased 13x9-in. baking dish. Sprinkle with cake mix and cheese; dot with butter. Drizzle with caramel topping and sprinkle with pecans. Bake until golden brown, 45-50 minutes. Let stand 10 minutes. Serve warm, with ice cream or whipped cream if desired.

½ CUP 347 cal., 17g fat (8g sat. fat), 29mg chol., 373mg sod., 48g carb. (29g sugars, 3g fiber), 3g pro.

TEST KITCHEN TIP

Don't leave out the cheddar! It adds a subtle sweet-salty flavor that makes this dump cake special.

MAMA'S BLACKBERRY COBBLER

Alabama has some tasty fresh berries. Several decades ago, my mama was going to pick blackberries to make a cobbler, but she went to the hospital to have me instead! This wonderful dessert is her mama's recipe.

—*Lisa Allen, Joppa, AL*

PREP: 15 MIN. • **BAKE:** 45 MIN. • **MAKES:** 6 SERVINGS

½ cup plus 2 Tbsp. melted butter
1 cup self-rising flour
1½ cups sugar
1 cup 2% milk
½ tsp. vanilla extract
3 cups fresh or frozen blackberries

1. Preheat oven to 350°. Pour ½ cup melted butter into an 8-in. square baking dish. In a small bowl, combine flour, 1 cup sugar, milk and vanilla until blended; pour into prepared dish. In another bowl, combine blackberries, remaining ½ cup sugar and remaining 2 Tbsp. melted butter; toss until combined. Spoon over batter.

2. Bake until topping is golden brown and fruit is tender, 45-50 minutes. Serve warm.

¾ CUP 491 cal., 21g fat (13g sat. fat), 54mg chol., 421mg sod., 75g carb. (56g sugars, 4g fiber), 5g pro.

EASY DOES IT

As an alternative for 1 cup of self-rising flour, place 1½ tsp. baking powder and ½ tsp. salt in a measuring cup. Add all-purpose flour to measure 1 cup.

LAZY-DAY DINNERS INDEX

ALPHABETICAL INDEX